My Name is Also Freedom

Shari Ho with Melodie Fox

My Name is Also Freedom
The Shari Ho Story

Copyright © 2018 Shari Ho, Melodie Fox,
Square Tree Publishing

Published by Square Tree Publishing
www.SquareTreePublishing.com
ISBN-13: 978-0-9988328-9-0

FIRST EDITION

Cover Design: Cathy Arkle—The Thumbprint group
Interior Format: Cheri Lasota
Cover Photo: Melody Welch
Author Photo: Anna M. Flores
Line Editing: Monica Bosque

For more information, please contact:

info@squaretreepublishing.com

For bulk orders of 10 books or more, contact

Square Tree Publishing at info@squaretreepublishing.com

Square Tree Disclaimer

The story you are about to read is based upon the true-life events of Ho Hsiao-feng, aka 'Shari Ho'. This narrative includes her memories, to the best of her recollection, as a young native Paiwan child of Taiwan, being sold as a slave, her abuse at the hands of her captors, both in Taiwan and the United States, and her subsequent escape and life in the United States.

The names have been changed to protect the privacy of those involved in the surrounding events. In no way is this story written to place blame or to single out those who played a part in Shari being sold as a slave or in her mistreatment, nor is it intended for her or others to profit from these events, but rather to shine a light on the plight of human trafficking survivors and the crime of human trafficking that still exists today. This story is meant to promote awareness and to encourage those who suspect a person is involved in the crime of human trafficking to speak out about such suspected activity; and to teach forgiveness and healing to survivors of such crimes, and to bring healing to all.

Dedication—Shari Ho

I dedicate this book, my story, to my publisher and good friend, Sherry Ward. You made this happen. Without you, my book would never have been written. God sent you to me. You worked so hard and were so patient for years for me to trust you to do this. You have helped me work on my education—everything! You were especially there for me in Taiwan. I want you to know that you have not only made my dream come true, but the dreams of so many survivors out there who have not had their stories told yet. My story is their story. Thank you so much!

Dedication—Melodie Fox

I dedicate this story to a young man I met who, after telling him about Shari Ho and what I was doing to get her story out there, felt the courage to tell me his own story about how he was also mistreated at the hands of an old lady who tied him on a leash when he was a small boy as her slave. His story of escape will be forever etched in my mind. I had seen this man so many times, having no idea what he had gone through. Many people out there have such horrid stories but find the courage to speak out when one survivor speaks out.

I dedicate this story to Cesar. God bless you, Cesar. You are not alone. Your voice gives courage to another. Thank you for encouraging me to keep pushing through my writing and for sharing a part of your story with me.

Table of Contents

Section III

Recommendations

"This story goes deeper into the heart and humanity that binds law enforcement with those whom we protect."

—Special Agent, Homeland Security Investigations

"Shari Ho's story was as heartbreaking to learn as it was compelling to read about. Melodie Fox retold her experience and found Shari's voice with a straight forward sort of compassion that managed to convey the horrific reality while showing her undeniable resilience. Shari's life as a slave to a heartless and calculating Old Lady was not enough to destroy her spirit and faith in God. Through the tears I felt hope. And just as I was feeling disappointed in all those who could have helped Shari during her desperate journey, I was inspired by those who ultimately stepped in and committed themselves to her freedom. A non-stop read, Melodie Fox channeled the inner voice of Shari such that you felt like you were there alongside her, trapped, enraged, hopeful, free.

This book is a must-read for anyone looking to understand more about the reality and dynamics of modern-day slavery."

—Brenda Wells, Founder i-5 Freedom Network

"I love that this book showcases both Shari's compassion for others and her incredible sense of justice. She has an important voice and I am so glad to have gotten to observe her become "Shari.""

—Amy Henry

Former case manager and
Anti-Trafficking Director,
The Salvation Army

Preface

The coffee shop was buzzing with people on this warm sunny day. I found a place outside to sit and pulled two more chairs up close to the heavy wrought iron bistro table that sat facing the parking lot and all the oblivious shoppers who walked past me on the sidewalk. I was waiting, excited and apprehensive, as the opportunity to help write an incredible story was within walking distance from me. Hsiao-feng, or 'Shari', as I would come to know her, would soon be here to meet with me. I had heard of stories like Shari's happening all over the world, but here in my hometown? As I soaked in the sunshine, I closed my eyes and let my mind wander. Quietly, questions rose to the surface.

"What were you thinking? How on earth are you going to do this? You've never written something like this in your life!" I shooed the thoughts away with a wave of my hand and said aloud, "That sun is getting hot!" My publisher, who was a good friend of mine, had met Shari after hearing her speak at her church. Human Trafficking was the night's theme and Shari's story had made quite an impact upon her. Sold by her parents in Taiwan at the tender age of seven, and spending over twenty years as a slave, Shari finally wound up in the U.S. Now, after nearly a year of encouragement and much prayer,

Shari agreed to let us both help her write her story. So much had been withheld from Shari while she was a slave all those years—she was never allowed to go to school, so speaking and writing her own language, as well as English, was very limited; and she had never learned how to drive. We chose a meeting place close by, as she was walking to the coffee shop from her apartment, which was just a few minutes away.

"What do you want to drink?" my publisher queried as she headed inside to pick up our drinks after receiving a quick call confirming that Shari was on her way. "Coffee, what else?" I joked as I reached for my digital recorder. I set it down on the table and shut my eyes once more. My thoughts returned to the monumental task before me. *Could* I really do this? I didn't know much of Shari's story but what I did know was intense enough to make me doubt whatever writing skills I thought I had. The noises from the street were interrupted and my thoughts were pushed aside as the small frame of a woman came in to view. Her smile was as bright as the sun and brought a warmth that melted my apprehensions. "Hello," she said smiling as she reached out her hand, taking mine in a gentle handshake. "I just live across the street," she concluded. I offered her a seat, her back facing the busy parking lot and the impatient people hurrying to do their Saturday morning shopping. Just moments later, all three of us sat sipping our drinks and the introductions began.

What I thought would be an initial meeting sprinkled with small talk and preliminary business loose ends, suddenly became a spellbinding tale of treachery, abuse, and unanswered questions. I had found myself transported, along with Shari, back to her past, descending through a dark door into a colorless world, leaving that warm sunlit morning behind. I was glad I had brought my recorder.

And this is how it began: me and my recorder, sitting with Shari, for sometimes up to three hours or more at a time, listening to her story, asking her questions, seeing the tears, watching her heart break once again. But as I listened and then transcribed each session, I heard through the pain a strength, a tenacity behind it all; a voice speaking out for others—not a voice of just a survivor or victim—but a voice of one who learned to fight and who looks forward to the fight to help others.

I felt at times the person of Shari was many personalities in one: the tears and pain showed her vulnerability, the child who longed for a family and wished only to be loved; as she talked about the survivors' meetings she pioneered, the advocate emerged, the hero, the one who would fight and exhort others to live beyond their captivity; and finally, the loving sister and daughter, wanting only to do what was best to keep her family together in unity of spirit. Her diverse personality was reflected in the many names she was known by: 'Lunlun' the name her mother called her, born as Paiwan Tribe member; 'Hsiao-feng', the Taiwan native, sold as a slave; 'Sharon', the name by which her captors called her when she was forced to move to the United States; 'Isabel', the name she tried to hide behind when the CNN story broke, and finally, 'Shari', the name she chose, becoming the strongly independent

American, now living in freedom. I saw the cultures mix and clash and blend into the unique woman who truly is Shari Ho.

I won't lie. These were all challenges for me. Understanding the Asian mindset, putting myself in Shari's shoes as she was mistreated, forsaken, and at times, angry at God. I wrestled, wrote and rewrote, and wrestled some more. My desire was for the voice of this brave woman to come forth regardless of cultural or language barriers. And with the encouragement of those I interviewed, I hoped I was indeed the right one to do this, and that the approach and path I took would be genuine.

It would be over 40 interviews later, countless hours of internet searches, lots of Skyping with family members, visits to locations, combing through piles of paperwork, documents, police reports, and an eye-opening trip to Taiwan before the book would be near completion. What you are about to read is my journey inside of Shari—and her journey to find her voice, herself, and a name that was uniquely hers—Shari Ho, no longer a slave, for…Her Name is Also Freedom!

—Melodie Fox

Acknowledgements

Shari Ho

There are so many who have helped me along the way, not only to be where I am today, but to see that my story was written. A few are listed here, and the many others I want to thank are listed at the end of the book. All of them have become good friends, and some I now call my family; your names have been changed to protect your privacy, but nothing can change how much you mean to me. Thank you so much!

Judy

Judy, you saved me from a life of abuse and enslavement. For that I will never be able to repay you. You are truly like a mother to me and I look up to you each day. I love you, Mom.

Lucy

Thank you, Lucy, for being my case worker. You had so much patience throughout my journey. You understood what I was going through, even when I didn't say a word. You literally saved my life! I will forever be grateful to you and that special day you were there for me.

Amy

Thank you, Amy, for being my very first case worker when I was free. You were the only one I could trust at the time. You encouraged me and were always there for me through the tough times.

Mimi

Thank you for your years of friendship. It is an honor and a privilege to have you by my side and helping all the other survivors who need help. You are a true friend.

Sister Marianna

You are like a mother to me. You taught me how to do some of the simple things in life. Even though I had to learn to adjust to the 'normal' world and would have outbursts like a stubborn daughter, you were always there for me. Thank you for your patience and love as you supported me each step of the way.

Cindy

I have no words to express how much you mean to me. Through all my ups and downs you have never given up on me. You are a true godly friend, sister, and mother to me. I will forever be grateful for all you have done for me!

Melodie Fox

Thank you, Melodie, for writing my story. I didn't know at first if I could trust you, but over time as I got to know you, I knew in my heart you were the right person to trust with the most important thing I had—my story. In Taiwan we became much closer. I like you more than stinky tofu—well almost—stinky tofu is just so good!

Acknowledgements

Melodie Fox

I would like to thank Sherry Ward—my publisher, my friend, and long-time prayer partner—for giving me the opportunity to write this book. She had the confidence in me that I was the right one to take on this daunting project, the one to bring Shari's voice to the written page. I am grateful to her for believing in my skills and in praying for God's anointing to be on my every word.

I would like to thank Shari Ho for opening her heart and trusting me to tell her story. She did not hold back, even the most difficult memories, but invited me in to those dark places with her. I will always cherish our first trip to Taiwan, shopping in the street market—me, holding all of her veggie and meat-filled bags, going from vendor to vendor, with such excitement, her wanting to cook a traditional meal for us. Of all the places we visited, some held dark memories, yet she was brave to face them all. This trip was filled with so many new memories, that it chased the old ones away for good. Thank you for this memorable experience that I will never forget.

I would like to also thank all of those I interviewed, those so instrumental in Shari's life and story. You were so helpful and encouraging to me. I could not have done this without you; especially Sister Marianna, who looked at me across from where we were sitting for the interview and said, "I believe you are the right one to do this story with Shari." Those words would never leave me, and I desperately needed them when I felt overwhelmed and inadequate for the challenge ahead of me. Thank you, all!

And thank you, Jesus! For, "Every good and perfect gift is from you, Father of lights…" I simply said, 'yes' to this task, not knowing all that lay ahead, but you were with me, leading me always. You worked out so many details that left me speechless, renewing my faith in miracles, time and time again. What you did on that Taiwan trip was beyond miraculous. There is no corner of the world that you are not at work in. May my eyes always be open to what you do on stage *and* behind the scenes!

Acknowledgements

Square Tree Publishing

Square Tree Publishing would like to thank the Human Trafficking Task Force whose dedicated team of community volunteers from law enforcement, victim service providers, non-profit organizations, faith-based organizations and government entities, make happy endings like Shari Ho's possible. Hours and hours of tireless hard work and tremendous love are given to victims of human trafficking to ensure they become not only survivors, but successful individuals who can go on to lead meaningful lives. Our sincerest 'thank you,' for all you have done for Shari and countless others.

We would also like to thank the following for their help in bringing Shari's story to these pages: Former Taiwan Minister of Foreign Affairs, Timothy Yang, Congressman Ed Royce, Special Agent from U.S. Homeland Security, and The Salvation Army. A special thank you to Cindy for all the tireless hours she has put into helping the Square Tree team get this story to fruition. This story would be unwritten if it wasn't for your encouragement and help.

"It takes a village to raise a child, but…
it takes a whole community to save one."
—Sherry Ward
CEO, Square Tree Publishing

Shari Ho with Melodie Fox

Introduction—Shari Ho

I am a survivor of human trafficking. I feel I am lucky. I am strong and stubborn. It's hard to speak about it. It is so very hard. At times, I don't want to think about it, yet it's the speaking that makes me stronger. I feel deep inside that I should do something for others. The past is the past, but I am concerned for others that have been in my situation. How will they survive? Some have children. How will they eat? How will they pay the rent? The beginning of being free is always tough.

All of my family still lives in Taiwan. We grew up very, very poor. People looked at us and thought, "Slavery."

I want to do something to redeem all of this, to make them all proud. My mom and dad never really finished school. I was never allowed to go to school. I can speak Taiwanese, Mandarin and some English, though. But I was determined to tell my story in the face of all this.

When I escaped from that life, I chose not to stay in a shelter. Maybe I could read and write by now if I did. It was my choice. But at that time I wanted to be free. I didn't want to have to depend on others for my needs anymore. I wanted to live free. This is my story. It is a journey that is still not complete but continues moving forward with each day. I am so thankful, so very thankful, to God for how He has turned all of my tears to joy and all of my sadness to rejoicing. I have been through so much but at each turn I can see how God was with me, leading me and helping me to be who I am and where I find myself today. I had looked forward to the day I would share this story with you. It has been my passion for so long to write this book and to be a voice for others, those who are survivors of what I have been through and much more. So many people saw what was happening to me but never said a word. It is time to speak out, to no longer be silent! This is not right, to sell another human being, to mistreat a Child of God, to watch and do nothing. This is MY voice speaking on behalf of them all. I need you to speak out with me so our voices can be strong. God is with us. He is always with us.

If you suspect a person is a possible victim of human trafficking please call:

National Human Trafficking Hotline
888-373-7888

Suddenly, Isabel

"Isabel's Misery Touches Taiwan"

—CNN Freedom Project Nov. 23, 2011

"While the melodrama continues to unfold on prime time TV, is Isabel really Hsiao-feng? Why does she not call her family back in Taitung? Is she angry with them? If she was living in poverty why was she carrying a designer handbag…? Are there any more twists in the story? No one seems to care about the fundamental question, which is why all this happened in the first place."

—The China Post, Nov. 29, 2011

This was the news story that swept the nation of Taiwan. A young indigenous Taiwanese girl is sold by her impoverished family to a wealthy woman to be an indentured servant. She longed to return, to find her family again.

When we met with some publishers, hoping to make a connection in the Asian market with Shari's story, one of them said, "Why do you think this story should be published? There are so many girls this kind of thing happened to, what is so unusual, so special, that people in China, Taiwan, should care to read it? The selling by the poor of their children, although not something that people do out in the open today, but once did so often, this story has been told. It is not unique. Why does this girl think such a story will impact anyone?" This question seemed odd to us, as Americans, but we heard this question again and again, 'Why her story'?

Why *is* Shari's story special? She wasn't sold into the sex trade—molested horribly, hooked on drugs, scarred inside and out and left for dead, like so very many. Even Shari's own sisters, who have tasted some of this same bitter life ask, "Why is your story different than mine, than anyone's back in that day?"

That was when the Bible story of Joseph came into my mind. Was it a strange thing to be sold as a slave in Joseph's time? The Midianites who bought Joseph without hesitation, were not afraid of breaking the law, it seemed. It was not the number one sin in those days. He was sold and taken to a town which had a boatload of slaves that were being 'auctioned off.' Did that city seem to frown upon this? No. And Joseph—along with all of those young boys (and girls, too, I'm sure) were sold again to the highest bidder. Joseph ends up as a penniless slave—unlike Shari Ho—and sets about working, doing household chores. He does them so well, and with God's favor, gets promoted. Unfortunately, Shari was not promoted, but God is at work behind the scenes to eventually bring her to America.

Joseph, however, feels the sting of being wrongly accused and is thrown into another pit—the bottom of a prison. I guess now we can see the comparison to Shari a bit more at this time. Sleeping on a cold hard floor, scraps of food for sustenance, probably hearing more than an unkind word or two towards him, it would be his persistence and his trust that "God would bring a better day, for I had a vision of such a day," that would finally put him on top. "Through faith and patience we inherit the promises," the Word of God says. Ok, but there still is the question of 'What is so special here? Why *this* story? Why Shari's story? Why Joseph's, for that matter?

Joseph's happily-ever-after was NOT in becoming 'Second-in-Charge' in all the land, nor of marrying the Pharaoh's daughter. It was being in the right place at the right time. It was forgiving his brothers for what they had done. It was being put in position to save his family—HIS PEOPLE—from what was coming.

Shari was taken to America—not just any place. She learned to forgive in spite of everything and took that message with her. She spoke that message out, wanting to find her mom again, her mom who sold her into slavery, her mom who left her in the care of abusive strangers. Shari is in the right place at the right time, and with the right message: forgive them. She brings a message that is unusual: grace and mercy towards her captors, forgiveness for them and for her family. Will her family be saved by this message? Will her family take in the food of forgiveness and grace, and grow and live in love? Joseph's family finally did. They welcomed it as they welcomed the grain that filled their stomachs in the famine that destroyed the land that was once known as 'the land flowing with milk and honey.'

Why this story? Why now?

Because God Almighty has a plan. He had it from the beginning, to save, to heal, to deliver, and to bring Himself into the lives of the Taiwan—and the Paiwan people!

Section I

Chapter 1

Media Frenzy

"Hsiao-feng, Hsiao-feng...Here...Look over *here!*" Voices shouted my name from every direction, temporarily muffled only by the explosions of light from cameras everywhere. I waved and smiled graciously, even though I couldn't see a thing, certainly not the faces of those calling to me from all different directions. The flashes were blinding. I held on to the railing and carefully began my decent, feeling my way down the stairs. There must have been forty or fifty reporters waiting for us when we arrived at Taiwan's Taoyuan International Airport. The wool knitted cap and dark sunglasses I wore provided little privacy from the overwhelming attention I was now getting from everyone and everywhere I went. They were at least somewhat of a shield against the onslaught of people, desperate to get a glimpse of the woman whose face had been all over the news for months.

"News that a Taiwanese woman who was
forced into domestic servitude in the U.S...made

headlines around the nation, and has led, as
expected, to wide coverage in local media."
—*China Post*, November 29, 2011

When I had finally decided to make the difficult decision to travel back to Taiwan, the country that I had been sold as a slave in, it was because of the kindness of Timothy Yang, the then Taiwanese Minister of Foreign Affairs and Vice-Chairman with the Taiwan Foundation for Democracy. My story had already become big news in Taiwan. I had no idea that agreeing to do a story on human trafficking for CNN's Freedom Project would catapult me to a household name in the country of my birth. Within days after it aired, I had reporters on my doorstep, but when the story reached Taiwan, the whole nation seemed obsessed with me, engrossed in my plight. I was the Jaycee Dugard of Taiwan! Her suffering had eclipsed my twenty years of captivity, but my fame spread throughout Taiwan just the same. Daily news stories about me appeared in the headlines and those claiming to be my sisters were on the news, tears in their eyes, holding up pictures of their long-lost sisters.

Such a commotion developed that the Taiwanese government joined the frenzy, to the point of offering to reunite me with my family, even paying for a DNA test to be sure—and only if I wanted a reunion. I wasn't sure at all at that time. When the CNN piece aired in November of 2011, fear of going back to a place that held only the saddest of memories for me had paralyzed my decision. Why would I want to go back?

I hadn't lived with my family since I was seven years old. The Old Lady I became a slave to had told me my family didn't want me; that no one did. She had said, "I paid a good sum of money to them for you. No one wanted you; no one will ever want you. You want to go back to them? Then pay me what I spent on you! You have been sold to *me.*" No, I could never go back. These thoughts stirred up the battle in me that I had all of my life: the love I had for my family, to forgive and be reunited with them, and the wrenching pain of feeling betrayed and neglected by the ones I wanted to love me the most. I had told the CNN reporters I wanted to see my mother, tell her how much I really loved and forgave her, but could I?

Somehow the news that my mother had become seriously ill reached me. Could now be the time to face my past? I felt the sincerity in his voice when Foreign Minister Yang talked with me about my mother. Moved by the CNN report, he graciously made a stopover on his way to El Salvador, Central America, to meet me. "If you want to go back to see your mother, that is something I can arrange. I can help," he assured me. Later he told the China Post, "We have to verify carefully. We don't want to have more damage to her feelings so I will do my very best and will ask my colleagues back home...to help me make sure it's the right family she's looking for...her story has touched our people deeply...but now my government and my ministry will do our very best to help her." By the time things were arranged I was amazed at the generosity of all of the people who clamored to help in some way...the Ministry of Foreign Affairs (MOFA), Taipei Economic and Cultural

Office, Council of Indigenous Peoples of Taiwan, and China Airlines, their selfless work in expediting visas and travel documents, even our airline tickets and all of our travel expenses were paid for—complete with bodyguards for protection taken care of as well.

As we all headed to the airport, the media firestorm had been lit. We pushed and squeezed our way through security, for the media had already arrived, trying to get a jump on the breaking story. I had some time to think about what would happen when we landed. Fourteen and half hours on that long flight across the sea, I hoped that I could at least sleep a little and be mentally prepared, have my wits about me by the time we descended into Taipei.

> *"...A Taiwanese woman who was identified in a CNN Freedom Project report on human slavery last November, left...Tuesday to return to Taiwan for a family reunion..."*
> —*Focus Taiwan*, January, 2012

It had been a long time since I had traveled to Taiwan. I had made this trip before, when I was still serving The Old Lady. Her Daughter had lived in the U.S. for some time and of course it was rare that The Old Lady would let me out of her sight, especially now that I was older. I had accompanied her then and eventually returned to live with her and her Daughter's family in the U.S. permanently, to wait on The Old Lady, hand and foot. My mind wanted to pull me back to that horrible time. I couldn't let it, so I reached for some headphones just as the inflight movie had started and turned up the volume, hoping to drown out those toxic images from poisoning me once again. My breath had already begun to quicken and waves of anxiety pulsed in spasms.

"Would you like something to drink, Miss?" the flight attendant asked softly in Chinese as she gently touched my arm. I abruptly pulled the headphones down over my neck and stared at her blankly. She spoke to me again, this time in English. "Something to drink?" she repeated slowly. "Yes... thank you..." I stuttered. This timely conversation was enough to reset my mind. The panic faded and my breathing returned to a deeper, calmer rhythm, not as shallow as it had been. I took a drink of the cool liquid and put the headphones on again. I told myself not to think too far ahead. I enjoyed the distraction the movie had given me, and when it was over I busied myself listening to my friends talk. I even managed to fall asleep for a few hours.

Awakened by the groans and grunts our plane made as it signaled its decent into Taipei, I felt a sudden surge of nervous energy. I still had time to freshen up somewhat and gather my thoughts. The announcement was made by the pilot to prepare for landing and I fastened my seatbelt. "Here we go..." I said, mostly to myself. The plane jerked and rumbled and hissed, touching down, almost as if uncomfortable now to be on the ground once again, bound by land and gravity, no longer free. I felt the same heaviness, back to reality once again. But I knew it was the sign of my first victory: I was back in

Taiwan. I had made it over the first hurdle of my homecoming.

As we cautiously disembarked from the long flight from the U.S. to the homeland I hadn't seen for years, I felt slightly sick inside, partly nervous at the attention, and partly because I wasn't sure how I would feel, seeing my family again and everyone knowing what had happened to me and why I was returning. I pulled my scarf around my neck and draped my coat over my arm. I knew January was one of the colder months in Taiwan, but the year-round weather is nearly always mild. I felt cold just the same. My stomach turned and all my muscles tightened as the cargo door groaned, slowly opened and the passengers began to spill out. I gather my belongings and made my way towards the opening. One by one, my entourage and I stepped out of the plane. The sun had set but I wasn't sure I wanted to shed my sunglasses just yet. I pulled them up towards my forehead and looked out into the night. Here I was. I was home. I was free. I was scared. I wasn't alone on my journey; half a dozen of those I had finally come to trust as friends were here with me. I felt the hand of Sister Marianna on my shoulder as if to say, "You can do this." Nodding in her direction, I breathed the fragrant air of my homeland in deeply and took my first step purposefully towards my healing.

"How does it feel to be back in Taiwan? What was it like, living in the U.S? When will you see your mother? Are you angry at all that has happened to you?" Like bullets fired rapidly from guns in all directions, the questions exploded towards me one after another as I took each step towards the voices and closer to facing my past. With media and reporters everywhere, the questions continued, even without a word of acknowledgement from me; some in English, some in Chinese but all them incessant. They continued to shout questions, many now using my Chinese name. A slight panic rose up in my heart. "Hsiao-feng, Hsiao-feng, what do you have to say?...When will you see your mother?...Tell me..." "Hsiao-feng, Hsiao-feng...Here...Look over *here!*" Those voices, calling a name I hadn't heard in so many years. How did they all know who I was? I was calling myself Isabel, the name I had used in the CNN report to conceal my identity, and yet my real name was being broadcast throughout the airport as if I were a pop star. This moment felt unreal. "How on earth did they find out my real name?" I whispered under my breath.

> *"A Taiwanese woman who was forced into*
> *domestic servitude...CNN's story, the tragedy of*
> *Isabel...has now been identified almost certainly*
> *as Ho Hsiao-feng from Taitung..."*
> —*China Post Online*, January, 2012

My lawyer had insisted on accompanying me. He was one of a string of many fighting for me pro bono, as my case came to court, and supporting me now that legalities had all but left me silent. And of course, there was Sister Marianna. Years prior, I had made Sister Marianna promise me she would come along, if ever I returned to Taiwan. Sister Marianna was a volunteer who found her way to working with the Human

Trafficking Task Force after viewing a moving video about a young Chinese human trafficking victim. She knew she had to do something to help. She had been involved with the Sisters of Saint Joseph, and there met one of my case managers. I spoke very little English, so Sister Marianna, fluent in both Mandarin and English, was a godsend both to me and the newly formed Task Force.

I remembered how she laughed when I had talked about finding my mother one day. "How will you find your mother in a country you haven't lived in for so long and were never allowed to travel in by yourself before? The Chinese language is the same when written, but not when spoken. One Chinese word can be pronounced so many different ways! How are you going to do this? Will you walk from place to place saying to everyone, 'Are you my mother? Are YOU my mother?' like the baby bird from the child's story." Sister Marianna had a stern but loving demeanor in the way she talked to me. It made me feel safe to be with her, knowing deep down inside she had the inner strength I could trust; there were no pretenses or lies with her. "I will go," she committed finally, "if you decide to return to Taiwan to look for your mother, I will be with you." She had kept her word.

Sister Marianna was from Hong Kong and had traveled the world, living in Canada and the U.S. because of her religious calling. I leaned heavily upon her savvy and language skills. As our group slowly made our way forward, I felt her hand reach out towards my shoulder, silently letting me feel her presence once again. I took a deep breath in and forcefully pushed it out. I felt like I was running a marathon in slow motion. Surely the 'thump, thump, thumping' of my pounding heart could be heard by those around me. Pushing, shoving, I could barely move through the crowd as hands grasped at my clothing. My hand reached for Derrick's, my long-time fiancé who had also come along on my quest. I had met Derrick before I was able to speak much English, but somehow felt secure and safe with him. He was a big teddy bear of a man—silent, unthreatening, unresisting. As my fingers stretched to grip his, he was pulled back towards the back of our entourage, sucked in by the power of the sheer volume of people. At least Derrick would be behind me, still there. It seemed our relationship was like that a lot, Derrick always being a few paces behind me, but never truly having 'my back.' I hoped this trip would change things.

We continued to navigate our way towards customs, through the moving walkway, past busy travelers, pushing and pulling their luggage, unaware what was happening. I kept smiling as the interrogation of the reporters who continued to follow us never skipped a beat. Out of the corner of my eye I observed my case manager, Amy, using her arms to form a barrier from the over-zealous media who tried to break into our little group. Amy had been the first person I had truly trusted. As my first case manager, I met her just three days after escaping my captors. She was such a source of strength to me, my buffer between the harsh new world I entered into when I escaped, and my fearful past. I don't know what I would have done without her. She had graciously come along to help and support me on this trip. She had been there at the very beginning of my journey to freedom and was here now, another wonderful angel from the Human Trafficking Task Force. Amy had taught me about American money, shopping, and budgeting. She labored at providing me the papers I needed to work in the U.S., as well as housing, a stipend and getting my life on the right track. We spent over a year together, me learning to trust her, and Amy, with a heavy caseload, making extra time to be my first real family.

A flood of thoughts spilled into my mind. I was glad, as the deluge blocked out the voices that still shouted for my attention. That person, Hsiao-feng, who I was in another time, a lost world, suddenly collided with this realistic world of wary strangers, caseworkers and friends. "Shari," whispered one of the bodyguards who kept the voices from coming too close, "Stay between us and we will lead you to the hotel safely." We were then greeted by Sun Ta-chuan, minister of the Council of Indigenous Peoples, and some MOFA officials, who fast-tracked us through immigration. I didn't answer any questions from reporters, but simply nodded towards them saying, "Thank you," in English.

Surrounded by my tenacious troupe and the two strong men who were assigned to keep me safe, we finally made our way through the crowd, my small, less than five-foot frame, unable to see anything but the head and shoulders of my guardian angels who were dedicated to protecting me, into the fresh, moist Taipei air outside the airport and towards the van that was waiting patiently for us. As we stepped outside I stopped and took a deep breath. I felt the damp air upon my face and heard the slight patter of light rain hit the covered overhang above me.

The evening sky lit up like day from cameras around me. I was so glad I wasn't alone on this trip. The large van stood at the curb, and the driver jumped out and swung open the doors, expertly filling his vehicle with our luggage. Climbing inside, I let out an audible sigh of relief and of excitement. Our first gauntlet, one of many, had been accomplished. I was here. I was back in Taiwan.

> *"Ho Hsiao-feng, the subject of a CNN report on slavery in November, has returned to Taiwan from the U.S...to be reunited with her family.*
>
> *Ho, confirmed to be a Paiwan aborigine from Taitung in Eastern Taiwan, arrived in Taiwan in the company of her friends, lawyer and U.S. social workers."*
>
> —*Taiwan Today*, January 19, 2012

I had arrived 'home' after being away nearly fifteen years, and separated from my family for over thirty. I had left, masked by lies, taken away from all I knew, never to have contact with my family or home again. Unknown, uncared for, insignificant. And now...not a person or TV station in my native Taiwan was not blaring my name. I was the center of a media frenzy. Every radio, newspaper, and television was competing to blare the winning top story...

*"Isabel's story of abuse sparked a media storm
in Taiwan…'This kind of humanitarian travesty
would not happen nowadays. I can assure you,
people in Taiwan are now much more human
rights conscious…today's Taiwan is different,'
said Taiwan's Foreign Minister, Timothy Yang.
CNN's Martin Savidge commented, 'For the
president of Taiwan himself wants to make
the reunion happen…the story has become a
sensation in Taiwan.'"*

—CNN, November, 2011

Once I longed for someone—anyone—to listen, to hear
my voice and rescue me, now a whole nation clamored to hear
what I had to say, to get a glimpse of me, to snap a picture of
the girl who was sold as a modern-day slave when she was just
seven years old...

Chapter 2

Humble Beginnings

Tucked between the luscious green mountains near Taitung and the beautiful blue waters of the Pacific Ocean lies the small quiet village of Dawu Township. Its warm wind-swept countryside curves along the highway that winds its way up and down the coast. Looking down from the grassy cliffs above to the ocean, small white-capped waves gently slap the shore below. Miles of endless sea spread out, a reminder of just how small we truly are in the vastness of life and how alone we can sometimes feel. Cold and indifferent to our struggles, yet oddly comforting, it flows on. This is the home of my people, the Paiwan. According to myth, this spot is where heaven is said to exist, and the Paiwan tribe (the name also means, 'human beings') have also chosen to live here for centuries. And although my memory of living here as a small child is vague, I remember the mountain hikes, the smell of the cool ocean breeze, and my mother cooking rice. I would find myself often dreaming of this 'heaven', a world lost to me. My own nation's history lost to me as well.

The majority of my tribe still lives here, along with other indigenous peoples of Taiwan, still clinging to the semi-rural living that has changed little over time. You will still see families choosing to cook and eat outside rather than in the small cramped hot and humid homes they live in. They sit and cook and eat and talk about life.

However, the clash of modern technology and communal living seems rather odd as family members crowd around several small BBQ's, cooking traditional meals, chewing the lip staining betel nut, all the while talking, texting, and checking out the latest posts on social media on their smartphones. Dogs roam about the narrow streets that lie just yards from the spacious main highway. Protected from most of the population and pollution of the big cities by the mountains and the sea, the days are mostly still and quiet, bridging perfectly the past and present.

Still dotting the mountainside are homes built with whatever supplies that may have been on hand at the time—corrugated scrap metal roofs, large rocks, tarps fastened by rope, which hold walls together, offering weak protection from the rain, along with odd items here and there—nothing that looked like building materials. These homes are much like the home I lived in with my family. But those are slowly disappearing as government funded homes replace them. Living, however, is still pretty simple: a shared bathroom and bedroom, small room to watch TV and large kitchen space that resembles more of a garage, having just the bare necessities such as a stove and sink. It is just enough, but no more.

Beds are still the long, flat tabled platforms rising less than a foot off the ground, piled with an enormous mattress, a little harder than the American in me would like to sleep on. I can remember sleeping, with most of my family, in those large flat beds, staring at the walls hoping the scorpions and snakes would not wriggle through to visit me while I slept.

Taiwan

Life is not as hard as it was in the early 1980s, at the time that I was born. Then, the poverty in my tribe was unbearable, especially for my father, who produced only female children. There is so much for me to still learn about—the history, the struggle of my people. I was not allowed to learn about my culture, any culture, when I was a slave. Returning to Taiwan in 2012, I began to learn about my country, about my tribe.

Our history is mixed with such poverty and heartache. In the faded memories I still see inside of me are the shadows of shame—being looked down upon—because we were so poor; looked down upon for being, 'from the mountain'; looked down upon as others saw only slavery. And why not? We were…slaves to the very poor life we led and of how others viewed our poverty. It was not always like this. The Paiwan were a brave and fierce people, whose tattooed hands and warrior skills put fear into all who would dare find themselves intruding upon their shores.

Taiwan (Formosa as it was known so long ago), was a beautiful gem desired by many nations. China would eventually lay claim to it, but it was the independent spirit of my tribe and other tribes that would provoke an invasion by the Japanese in 1874, leading to their ultimate domination in 1895. Aboriginal tribes such as my own Paiwan resisted the heavy-handed Japanese rule, which would last until the beginning of the 1930s, when China once again laid claim.

The Japanese colonization of the island was harsh. It began with an oppressive strict period of rule which eventually gave way, just after World War I, to a time where all peoples and races here were treated more 'equally' (proclaimed by Taiwanese Nationalists). And finally, during World War II, a period of Kōminka, a policy which aimed to turn the Taiwanese into loyal subjects of the Japanese emperor.

After World War I, Japan had begun to grow at such a rate it became desperately in need of resources for its people. Taiwan, with its fertile soil and abundant resources, met this need. The Japanese wanted to compete with the British Empire, hoping to make Taiwan its 'model of perfection' of all that could be done by them. Railroads were built, banks established, ports were completed for shipping, and electric power reached the island—and all this happened quickly. By 1905, Taiwan was considered the second-most developed region of East Asia and was financially self-sufficient, no longer in need of subsidies from Japan's central government.

Under the Pan-Asian beliefs of Governor Shimpei Goto, exports and food production increased by four times and by 1925, Taiwan was a major food supplier for Japan's industrial economy. The health care system was established, and infectious diseases were almost completely eradicated. As harsh as this rule could be, prosperity accompanied it.

It was during this time that a move to educate (more likely, indoctrinate) the Taiwanese, including all native tribes like my own, began. Mandatory education proved valuable to all Taiwanese, creating the importance of the written word even to today. World War II would see the Chinese regain Taiwan and by 1952 the transition would be complete.

My Father

It was this push by the Japanese to educate all of Taiwan that gave my father his education. Compulsory studies enabled him to read and write and he was the only one, to my knowledge, in our family who had been to school. But although this seemed to be a huge advantage to most, it would have no effect on me. My father was a complicated and often cruel man. I could not understand why he treated my mother so poorly, and as just a very young child, I felt a distaste for him, even in his kinder moments. He was an alcoholic and abusive. Maybe it was the fact that no matter how hard he tried he could not gain the respect of those in our village, or that he could bring in no steady income for our family, and he produced no sons. Whatever may have shaped the way he was, it was set in stone by the time I was born, the second of six girls. My father was never able to keep a job and it was my mother who provided most of the money to keep our family from starving. She worked as hard as she could but would never end up making enough to keep my sisters, including myself, from being sold off, generating enough money to barely keep those who remained behind enough to exist on. I was stubbornly defensive towards my father, seeing him drink and often fly into a rage, which was aimed mostly towards my mother. I felt strongly protective of my mother. I never felt love for or from my father. He seemed distant and mean and only later in life would I find out some of his dark past and reasons he turned to alcohol to numb his troubled life. Few fond memories have been buried deep, where I can now see his attempt to give us a better life, but of course then, I could not see it that way.

The TV

I remember once my dad had decided to get a TV for us. It was a luxury that was well beyond our means, but he brought it home one day and we were all thrilled! Why on earth had he thought of such an idea when probably meat or some food would've been more practical, I'll never know, but we were excited just the same.

I remember hearing the commotion outside as this grey-brown box was hauled into the house. I had been outside doing some chore or another when the loud shouts of excitement reached me. I ran up the path towards the house, my bare feet stirring up the loose dirt and carrying the small dust cloud I made upward, clinging to my already filthy legs. Tearing around the corner I stopped short, just in time to see my father and another man maneuver the TV through the doorway. I really had no idea what all this was about, but I was excited just the same. I pushed passed everyone, squeezing between a few legs to get a front row seat in front of this new thing. The box was a dark shiny brown with a grayish glass front, curved at the edges. We all crowded around the set, eager to see what most families took for granted.

I heard my father curse a few times as he looked for a place to plug it in. There were some buttons and dials on the right side of the glass screen and after managing to push past us girls, for we were all now so crowed in front of the box, he pulled on the 'on' switch. It took a moment or two before a faint blue-gray light formed from the edges and slowly filled the screen. My mother had joined us by now from the kitchen area, curious enough to see this contraption and a bit suspicious of how her husband was able to buy such an expensive item. The light glowing from the screen gave way to pictures jumping and changing with great streaks of color. And the sounds! Music and talking and laughter! We watched it all day and into the night, fitting in chores that had to be done in turn, so we wouldn't get into trouble. We all groaned when the fun was over and it was time to go to bed.

Early the next morning we heard a banging on our door. It was a man asking for my father. We heard arguing outside and then he barged in and unplugged the heavy TV set with an angry jerk and loaded it up on to his small pick-up truck. He was yelling at my father, scolding him saying, "How did you intend to pay for the thing when you had no money whatsoever?" He slammed the door of the truck, still mumbling complaints and took our lovely TV away.

My father had a hard life. I never really knew what had made it so hard, just stories about his past, some unfair things he had gone through. I never remember him having a job or going to work at all. He spent most of his time drinking. If he didn't drink, he would shake. He would often look for work, but no one wanted to hire him. I didn't know why he seemed so hated by the people in our village. He had worked at a furniture factory when he met my mother and it seems something happen that got him into debt. The story went that he had co-signed on a loan for a friend and his friend did not pay, which made him responsible for the debt. I don't know if the story is true, but it might explain why he struggled so with money.

Seeds of Bitterness

My father had also found himself on the wrong end of a lawsuit, which made him bitter. It was after this that his bouts of drinking grew so much worse and his abuse towards my mother increased. My mother later told me she believed that this was the beginning of selling us children as slaves for money.

Things seemed to get worse for my father and not better as time went by and survival was tough in those days. I think he blamed my mother for many of the problems we had. All I do know is his drinking would not solve things and would only lead to many more such problems. Once I over-heard an argument when mother was taking the washing off the clothesline. Why they were fighting I never did know, but a loud noise drew my attention towards the mountain. The wind was blowing the clothes that still hung on the line. They were flapping harshly in the wind. As they argued, my mother still pulled the clothes off the line, folded the dry ones in half and put them in the basket. She did not look my father in the eye. Suddenly, I saw my father kick my mother and I watched as she tumbled down the grassy hillside. I screamed as I ran to where she lay. Relieved to see just a few scratches, I looked back at this man with anger in my eyes. "Why you treat her this way?!" thoughts fumed inside. My mother was pregnant with my little sister at the time.

I would discover much later, that his out of control anger and drinking would play a big part in his death.

Hsiao-feng

I was named Hsiao-feng. There is a mythical royal bird in Chinese with a similar name. This magnificent bird is so gentle, benevolent and giving, it will not take from anyone; its food, only the dew of the morning mist. It appears only in places that are blessed with the utmost peace, prosperity and happiness, and it hides away in times of trouble. Maybe in an effort to bring hope to our harsh family life I was given this name. Many mornings as I awoke, I rushed to the door to see if the brightly colored bird had made his appearance, but

I found only the dew on the ground and the mountain mist hanging low along the path. The disappointment would not keep me from hoping to see it. I would remind myself to keep hoping and be positive. I try to always carry thankfulness inside of me. When I faced terrible times I think on what I am thankful for. I am thankful for having hope.

A Seed of Faith

It's funny how the struggles and the hardships of life can create a tenacity to survive that is almost miraculous. I only lived with my birth family for a short seven years, but I had a determined spirit in me that would not be crushed or stolen from me. I was just as determined to love as I was to hate, but I also had the wisdom to know that a life of hate could destroy me from the inside. How often I let the two battle within me, but peace of mind and love would always win—it seemed God would make sure of that. He spoke to me deep inside my heart. No one told me He would do this, or that He even existed, but His spirit was my guide, always keeping me on the right path in the darkest places of my life. Maybe it was my mother who planted that seed in me. She was the only one in our family who went to church. She believed in God and I was drawn to her faith.

Catholic Church

My mother went to Catholic Church at that time. Maybe it was these church visits that planted a seed of God in me.

In those days, I went with her. I loved going anywhere with my mother. We walked mostly or sometimes took the bus. It was just the two of us. How I wish I could remember the message or what we did in that church! I remember watching her, seeing her face, wondering what she was thinking. Voices echoed off the walls as the man up in the front talked. There was something peaceful about this place. It was over too soon and we would head home.

It's hard to explain but I knew that God was there somehow.

Chapter 3

Memories of Home

Family Life in the Village

The house I was born in no longer sits atop that grassy mountain cliff in Taitung. The government has done so much to help the tribes and reduce the poverty I knew as a child. More homes, rent free, are available and all of them have electricity and more modern comforts than I had then. Few, however, still perch there like mine did as a child, built with rocks and tarps and tires. The weather is pretty consistent year-round, mild, leaning more hot than cold, but we do get quite a lot of rain. During the typhoon season, which starts sometime in June and lasts into October, the rain just pours down. I can still remember the nights the rain dripped down on us from the cracks above our heads. We had so many leaks in our ceiling it was a wonder the roof didn't collapse! Sometimes during this season huge trees would fall to the ground, smashing whatever they fell upon. The water would shove leaves, mud, tree branches, anything in its path, forcefully like a river, down towards the road blocking it from any vehicle that tried to pass. Those in the village would work together—even my father—to dig the debris and thick mud out so the road would be clear again.

The rain would also bring out all the insects and creatures that were looking for a place to dry off. That's when the snakes would come into our house. I hated those snakes! They'd wriggle through the small holes they could find in the walls and curl up under the bed. And in the colder winter time, the snakes especially liked the warmth from the fire we made inside.

Once I was bitten by a poisonous ten-legged critter. I don't know what sort of bug this was; I just remember I had been sleeping as it crawled up on me. I don't know if I tried to swat it or what, but I felt a sharp pain as the creature bit into me. Of course, going to the doctor was out of the question. My mom simply made a mixture of rice alcohol and smashed ginger root, a messy wet mix, and put it on my bite. Oh, the pain was incredible! But it wasn't long after that the bite just disappeared. I felt like it was a miracle. God was protecting me. This is how we coped whenever we were sick; we just dealt with it ourselves. We did have people who would donate medicine to our tribe from time to time but when that wasn't available, we would rely on our own homemade remedies. Amazingly, we all lived and are healthy today.

Our house was pretty primitive and much too tiny for all of us. It had been built with electricity; we just never had the money to pay for it. Others around us did. Some used propane, but we used fire to cook and for light. We would use the natural sunlight during the day and firelight at night. In winter, it would get so smoky when we'd have a fire inside. My mom would collect the wood so we'd have it for the winter, stacking it up against a somewhat dry spot near the house. My sisters and I slept together on a flat wood platform bed with no mattress. We shared the pillows between us. Blankets were also donated to us. Our parents slept on the ground. Our house was super small. We had no bathroom in the house. If we had to use the toilet, we went outside somewhere and dug a hole.

I can't remember my oldest sister ever living with us. I saw her only twice, so really, I became the oldest one out of the rest of us five girls. I saw her only twice. I was helpful to my mom. I swept the floor—which was dirt but hard dirt. Sometimes we had rice. My mom showed me with her hands how much water to put in the big black pot so it wouldn't spill over and it would cook perfectly. I couldn't let the water come to a rolling boil and I must always keep a careful eye to watch the fire. The first time I cooked the rice I burnt it. I remember how bad I felt then. "This is what we have to eat," my mom said. I realized how important it was to pay close attention to all she taught me. I made a decision right then that I was never going to burn the rice again!

In the summer my dad would go hunting for wild pig, deer, rabbit (which I had hated the taste of), coyote and even small wild mice. He would go with most of the men from the village, hoping to get a generous 'kill shot,' for if you were the one who shot the head of an animal, you got the head, which meant a bigger portion for your family. In winter, we caught fresh fish from the ocean. The biggest problem for us was refrigeration. We had no way to keep the meat fresh so we had to salt it, hang it up, and dry it. A few meals of cooked fresh meat would be enjoyed and then more of a jerky would have to sustain all of us. We all shared. The village rule of sharing meant no matter who killed what, everyone enjoyed the spoils—which didn't always go too far. My mom used the fat from the animals that we hunted to make the oil to cook our vegetables in. I remember always eating sweet potato tops cooked in that oil. That's how we survived.

'Lunlun'

"Lunlun, Lunlun?" I can still hear my mother call to me. She had often called me this, my tribal name, when she was in a good mood; what it meant, I couldn't tell you. I always thought it had to do with my size, me being so little I stand barely five foot tall today, but whatever it meant, I knew it meant she loved me. And I loved my mother. She was always so hard working and generous. She cared for all of us girls and did the best she could in spite of our extreme poverty. "I want you to help me dig up some yams," she'd say. Yams were a regular meal for us. I remember my mother loved to share when her harvest was plentiful.

My Mother

My mother planted a garden each spring so our family would have food to eat. She had such good fortune working in the soil, for the things she planted seemed to love her and grew without much trouble. She would work hard to pull weeds and keep the vegetables from being eaten by various bugs and animals. Yams, sweet potatoes and corn; we all ate from that garden. I remember when it was time to harvest. My father, who did not help much at all in the planting or the harvesting, would see her pull up the root vegetables and the other produce and then she'd happily announce to the neighbors that she had plenty to share. He would question her generosity with a warning, "Why do you give to these judgmental people? You see how they treat us! You know that come winter time when you are in need, they will forget what kindness you've done for them and turn a cold shoulder to your lack!" He would finish with a snort and walk away. My mother would give an uncaring look in his direction, shrug her shoulders and say, "That's okay. I don't care what they do; when I have enough, I'll do it again and share, anyway." Nothing would stop my mother from giving when it was in her power to give. If she had it to give, she would, without complaining.

I can still see her feeding my sister, who was not well at the time and could not eat for herself. My mother put the food into her own mouth and would chew and chew, making it soft enough, then feed it to my sister so she could regain her strength. There were many hardships that came our way, but my mother always put us first when she could, and I know she wanted the best for us all.

The Sickness

"Something is not right…her head is so hot—she is burning up!" My mother told my father. "What am I to do?" he replied. "We have no money for a doctor…" his voice trailed off. I felt the panic in my mother's words, but I was too little to even respond, or to tell her how I felt. I was sick, very sick—I knew it, she knew it, too. I lay there not moving, my throat was so very sore, and I had a rash that covered my body. "Ma-ah-ma," I cried, but the sounds I made were mostly sobs and groans. The hours of cold wet cloths on my forehead seemed to do absolutely nothing. The year was 1986. My mother didn't know what to do. She had to work to support the family and any extra money, if there was such a thing, was certainly not there for hospital visits.

My mother had gotten work at the National Park at that time, as a cook and housekeeper for the people there, cooking for the workers. She would have to work a week at a time there and often had to take us girls, there were five of us at that time, with her to work. This could be so difficult. My mother often watched the neighbor children when they were in need of a babysitter, but they would never return the favor. "That man is a useless alcoholic," they'd say about my father. "Look at how they live!" However, my mother remained kind and generous and hardworking; she would simply carry my little sister, and the rest of us would walk to the mountain to help her work. It was around this time that I became so very sick. I think I was just about three or four years old at that time, when I suddenly developed a high fever, and itchy red spots that had slowly covered my tiny baby soft skin. My mother got us ready to leave to the mountain when she realized that I was too weak to walk myself. "You must help carry your little sister," Mama had told my one of my sisters. "I must carry Lunlun; she is too sick to walk." My fever had brought my temperature up so very high and nothing would bring it down. But my mother still had to work, or she would lose her job and we would not eat, so she wrapped me in a blanket and pulled me close to her. I felt so hot, but I let her pick me up and carry me like a bundle of sticks.

Bumping and jostling, I felt the trail under her feet as she carried me down the mountainside towards the road at the bottom. There was a woman, she was not of our Paiwan tribe, who owned a small shop at the bottom of the mountain. She had been sitting out front of her shop, drinking some tea, when my mother and my sisters came down from our home. It was this shop woman who brought the seriousness of the situation to the attention of my mother. My red, feverish face peaked out from under the blanket I was wrapped in. "What is wrong with your little girl?" the woman asked. She got up from her chair, setting her teacup down, and approaching us, carefully peeled back the bit of blanket that hid one of my cheeks. She gasped as she saw my condition. "This girl may have smallpox!" She exclaimed, as she looked back at my mother who had me in tow. I was sweating heavily now and was nearly lifeless-looking. She knew my mother was, 'from the mountain,' and couldn't afford the medicine to make me well. She stopped my mother, not letting her walk any further, urging her to take me to the hospital right away. After the woman persisted, I was taken to the doctor and given medicine to help bring the fever down and to fight the disease. The hospital bill was too much for my mother to pay, yet the shop woman didn't hesitate and insisted on paying it. The woman's kindness saved my life that day, and for that I am very thankful. My mother, however, had to work the hospital debt off.

Paying off the Debt

The shop woman had some property in which she raised deer and other animals that needed feeding. So to pay off the debt, my mother would climb to the top of the mountain where the wild grasses grew each day and cut down the tall shoots and haul the large bundles back down to her property. Many times after I was well, I climbed with my mother, up to the top where the tall grasses grew. We would cut them down together, stacking the piles high on our backs, and carefully climb back down to see to it that the animals had their fill. She did this daily for two years. I remember my mother had become pregnant at the time, so walking up the mountain and cutting the bundles of grass was especially hard work. After she would haul grasses for my debt, she would go to another job in order to provide for our family.

I recovered, but I have always been the smallest in the family—all of my sisters being so much bigger than me. I don't remember the lady who saved my life, nor my hospital stay, but I do remember those early mornings my mother got up before going to work, hauling grasses and such to feed this woman's animals. My mother never complained about doing this.

The Shoes

My memories come back from time to time of those early days, living on the mountain. They are often like the patches on a quilt of many different designs and colors, one here and one there, rarely in sequence. But when they come I try to grasp them firmly, not wanting them to float away. One day something brought back this memory of me with my mother, going to different places. I can see her face and how the hair fell across her forehead into her eyes. She would hold my hand as we walked towards the bus station. On the way home we saw the many people who sold things near the bus station. I curiously looked at vendor after vendor, when I spied a pair of sandals for sale; most of the time I ran around barefoot. These sandals were so pretty, dotted with brightly colored flowers. "Mama," I bravely asked, "Will you buy this pair of sandals for me?" Shoes were such an important thing to own; if you had shoes, you were not so truly poor.

Shoppers were buying all kinds of things on the street and I could hear their voices, asking, "How much for this?" or

"How much for that?" The little shopper in me came out right then and there. I knew that somehow my family was different, we worked so hard for the little we had, but I didn't truly understand what poor really meant. My mother gave a tug on my hand as she gently pulled me away from the vendor's wares. "If I buy a pair of sandals for you, Little One, then I need to buy a pair for all of your sisters." What she said hit me hard at that moment. I guess she was right, I hadn't thought about my sisters. It was only right to buy shoes for them, too. Turning my head back over my shoulder I took one last look at the sandals. They were so colorful and pretty. "I am thankful I have all of my sisters rather than having a pair of sandals," I thought aloud. "One day I will buy a pair of shoes for myself AND for my sisters." I consoled myself with this thought, something I would become very good at when I found myself far from my family and happiness.

The Apple

Once on another such trip my mother and I passed by a display of apples, stacked up in boxes, set up for sale. I looked down at the apples. I wanted to have one so bad! They looked so juicy and it was a hot day. Ripe apples filled the cart and the lady selling them reached out a hand to me with a sample of her wares. "Please, Mama, may we buy an apple, today?" I begged. My mother waved her hand at the vendor, which I knew meant, 'no.' Looking down at a bin which contained the apples the vendor couldn't sell—those bruised, pecked, slightly rotten on one side, my mother saw those discarded ones. The smell was not as pleasant, coming from the bin. Discarded leaves of vegetables, torn packing supplies, milky puddles from tofu vendors and other garbage lay nearby, strewn about. I glanced down as well to what she saw as she said to me, "We cannot afford to buy one of those apples, Lunlun," she said, nodding her head towards the lady, "but reach down there…in that bin…there is more than half of the flesh left on that apple in there; you may eat that." I looked at the apple in the garbage. I was hungry, so very hungry. I just kept looking into that garbage bin. I couldn't do it. The apples were spoiled, and I just couldn't bring myself to reach down towards them. Suddenly several dogs burst from out of nowhere, snapping at each other and starting to fight. Several boxes were knocked aside as they growled and tore into each other. My mother yelled at the dogs and jerked me away. The rotten apples rolled out onto the dirty street.

My Brother

I remember caring much for my sisters. My oldest sister was not at home so, as the second-oldest of our family, I was expected to look after my sisters. My mother did have sons from her first marriage and I do remember my older brother coming to visit. All of her sons were much older and did not live with us. It was usually me, and all of my younger sisters.

My older brother was very nice. I can only recall that he did visit every so often and when he did he always brought food— lots of food! I thought, "He is such a kind brother to bring all this food to us!" He would bring fruit and vegetables and even sometimes meat. I looked forward to his visits and remember thinking to myself, "I want to be this kind of a big sister to my family. One who brings gifts and helps them when they are in need." I remember my older brother always with love.

My Sisters

I was often in charge of taking care of my sisters when my mother and father were out. They would have to go to look for work and sometimes that would mean they would not be home for hours and, possibly, long after the sun had gone down.

My mother had taught me many things: to clean the house, wash the clothes, scrub the dishes, sweep the floor, and of course to cook and make rice. She also taught me how to make a fire. We didn't have a working stove at the time, so we had a place outside were we set up some rocks. My mother told me, "You find three rocks—make them into a triangle shape, so the pot can sit on it." I would set the wood just so and get it started. "If we come home too late, you must set the fire up and cook some food for your sisters." My mother would tell me. If she was really late, I was to have all the girls in the house and shut and lock things up and not to go outside again. I know my mother trusted me to do this. I was so little, but she knew I could do this.

I can remember one time when my parents were out looking for work and I was getting things ready to cook us dinner. I was caring for all four of my younger sisters then.

We had gone out and picked some wild vegetables from the garden. We rinsed the dirt off and I got the knife to cut them up for the pot. All of my sisters were sitting so close to me as I started chopping. "Chop, chop, chop…Oh, no!" I cried, as I cut into my 5th sister's hand with the sharp knife. I did not see a lot of blood, but the cut was very bad. I remember that she really did not cry much. Just then my mother and father came home. They saw what had happened and grabbed my sister up and took her quickly down to the doctor. She had to get stitches for that cut and she still has the scar on her hand to this day. My mother was not angry with me. She said, "You did your best." You know, there were so many times after I was sold as a slave that I felt hate towards my mom, but when I remember this I think, "My mom is not that bad. She really did teach me so many things in the short time I was with her."

The Mountain Lily

Living near the mountains would bring many tourists to the area and provide different jobs for my mother to work. She cleaned rooms and did other work to meet our family's needs. I remember once when she 'traveled to the mountain' she returned with a lily in her hand. Fields of them grew at one time, high up on the mountain top. This flower is so big and beautiful, a deep orangey-red and yellow, like the colors of the rising and setting sun, fiery, comforting, brilliant. She would say, "Close your eyes and stretch out both of your hands, Lunlun." I obeyed her as my tiny hands reached out towards her. I felt the moist pedals, tender and crisp and caught the faint fragrant scent. "Do you know what this means?" my mother asked me. I opened my eyes and looked at my beautiful treasure. It filled my two tiny hands, its long finger-like petals poured over my own fingers, yet I was careful not to drop it to the ground. "I do not know, Mama." I replied. My mother seemed rather serious about this answer as she stared into my eyes as if to say, 'this is very important, Little One, you must not forget this,' and said, "This flower, the Mountain Lily, is both beautiful and strong. It grows high up on this mountain. It takes me a long while to hike up far enough in order to find this lovely flower. I want you to be like this flower—pretty, yet strong. You must be *strong*." Then she continued, "This flower is not easily crushed. It withstands the rains and the harsh wind yet remains perfect, whole, pure and bright. Even long after I have picked it and made the long journey to carry it down to you, it remains big, beautiful strong."

Last Supper

I had just turned seven years old. I wish I could remember what day or what month it was, but I can't. When I left my family to live as a slave, that day would not be acknowledged in any way, so I never really knew how old I was for sure. It was not really the custom to celebrate a birthday or holiday that I could remember in my family, so I didn't understand what was happening when one day after my mother had come from the market, she began busily cooking an unusually large meal.

"Is tonight special?" I heard my 4th sister ask. There was no reply, but all of us girls, with the exception of my oldest sister, helped with the cutting of vegetables and the preparing of the food. We did not often eat all together. My mother was breastfeeding my youngest sister, who was still just a baby, and my mother, knowing there was never enough food for us all, always was the last to eat. Meat was not a regular dish for dinner, for it was too expensive or hard to come by. We didn't have enough money to buy and raise chickens, so it was a rare occasion we had meat like chicken. We all loved rice, which was also hard to come, but more often we ate a type of porridge instead, which I remember my mother made in a large pot. This was our usual dinner. But on this night we all sat together. The smells were incredible! For the first time I can remember chicken cooking away and rice— the largest pot of rice I have ever seen—steaming away. The delicious smells pushed the questions of 'why' or 'what' that had popped into my head earlier, far away. All I knew was this was how I wanted things to be always. 'Maybe things were changing. Maybe, the bad times were leaving, and new good times of chicken and rice were taking its place,' my heart hoped as I nearly spoke my thoughts aloud. I watched my mom as she took each piece of chicken and carefully wrapped it in a bitter leafy vegetable and placed in on a plate to serve to our family.

"Do you know why we are having this big meal with chicken and rice?" my mother announced, not expecting anyone to answer her question as she quickly responded to her own inquiry. "It is because your older sister is working hard, and this money she has earned has bought this feast for all of us." All my thoughts were on the meal and my family that surrounded the table. My heart was so full of joy as I thought of us being here as a family. There was food for us all and each could have plenty, as it should be. I did not know this would be the last meal I would ever eat with my family. This was the last time I would laugh and eat and feel full inside. It would be twenty years until I would lay eyes on most of those in this room again.

As I bit into the chicken it tasted bitter, for the herb surrounding it touched my lips. "Mama, something is wrong here," I said. "The chicken is no good. It is spoiling the meal," I announced, disappointedly. I remember the way my mother looked at me. It was a look I had not seen before. She was serious and seemed just a bit sad. How could she feel anything but happiness? We had such a feast in front of us and everything seemed perfect for once. After a moment, she spoke, but I did not expect the answer she gave. "Life is like this meal, Lunlun. It is sweet and good, but bitter and hard. Your life will be like this, too. Always be patient; endure and overcome because tomorrow will always be better. Beneath the bitter herb is tender meat, to make you strong. Do not stop at the first bite; keep eating. Tomorrow *will* be better. You must remember this meal. You must remember this night. And, remember my words when times seem too bitter to bear. Keep yourself strong with this thought."

We all ate and the meal was good. We ate and were full, but we ate with less joy after that. Something was different about this night. I think I knew things were never to be the same, although I was not quite sure why. But I always remembered what my mother had taught me that night. I closed my eyes, taking a picture in my mind of this night. I was determined to remember it; to remember what my mother had taught me that night.

Chapter 4

Take Me!

I have always had a deep love and longing for family. The memories I have of living with them in the beautiful green mountains of Taiwan are like small puffs of smoke that appear and are so real, but as I reach out to grasp them, they slip through my fingers. Many times, as I mindlessly went about the chores I had to do every day as a slave for The Old Lady, I would think about my family—not just the whys of how they came to give me up—but what had happened to each one of them—my mother and my sisters.

Although I was so small, I was fierce when it came to standing up for what was right. And I was very protective of my little sisters. I would see my parents fighting and jump right in, defending my mother and talking back to my father. How often he would chase me around, threatening to beat me if he caught me! I could not let a wrong go unnoticed. It would take years to get that fighter in me to come out again after my years of slavery, but it was in there, waiting for an injustice to rise, and me to rise with it.

The conversation is cloudy, but I remember talk of sending my little sister away, who was just a baby, no older than an infant at that time. They talked of selling her or 'adopting' her out, more likely for money, which was no different from selling her. My parents were arguing, like they did nearly every day. My father could be so violent. He would push and shove my mother, holding nothing back, until she was bruised or would fall to the ground. I heard them talking about my little sister. Were they planning on sending her away? I couldn't bear the thought of never seeing her again. What if she were to go to a home where they were mean to her, or worse? I felt my face beginning to feel hot with anger. If I thought I could, I would fight my father and not let him do this thing. But I was just a child. I knew he could hurt me or take it out on my sisters or mother. I heard someone calling my father from the doorway. I saw a man and woman standing just outside. Were they the ones who were coming to take my little sister away?

I saw her little face, such a precious little smile, as I scooped her up in my arms and quickly tried to find a place to hide. I ran as I looked for a place to hide us both. Could I find a cupboard or closet to climb into? Maybe behind the door? I frantically darted about but I knew it was useless as they easily found me. "Hand her to me," my father commanded, stretching his hands towards me. "She is so little," I said, trying to sound so bold and grown up. "Sell me first. Sell me." My anger turned to tears as I turned and faced my mother, still holding my baby sister tight, begging, pleading between the sobs, "Take me! Please—take me!" I would've rather been sent away than to see my little sister torn from me. "Please," I begged again and again, "Please don't sell her...sell ME!" My mom thrust her hands forward and tore my baby sister away from me and gave her to the couple. Although she tried to hide them, I saw the tears in my mother's eyes. I stood there, crying, watching my little sister being taken away by these strangers and my parents doing nothing to stop it.

My father jerked me away from my mother, pushing her aside, mumbling some insult at me and my mother as he spat on the floor. He grabbed me by the arm and forced me outside, yelling at me to be silent. He threw me to the ground. "You'll listen to me or else..." He started to tie me to a post that supported the overhang that shaded the house from the hot sun. There was a stick lying nearby that he snatched up to beat me with. My dad bent over me, hand raised to beat me with that stick while I struggled to get away. That is when I heard my mother warn him, "Ok...you do this, you know, she will need to go to the hospital. Do you have money to pay for this?" I felt my dad's angry grip relax a little as he stopped and stood up. A silent moment passed and then tossing the stick aside in frustration, he let go of me and walked away. I sat on the ground in a heap, still devastated that I would not see my little sister again. It wasn't but a day or two later that I would also leave my family forever. This battle I fought all alone, but I did not know that the war had only just begun. I thank God that the couple who adopted my sister treated her as their own daughter, and never a slave. I found this out later when I was reunited with my sister when I returned to Taiwan.

A Friend of My Father

There was a man in our village who had lost his job. He struggled, just like we all did, to earn enough money to feed his family. Most of the villagers found physical labor jobs, working hard; the majority of these jobs lasting only a week or two. This man in our village found something else, something that paid much more and required much less sweat or strength. This man was a friend of my father.

I will say that this man became a broker of sorts. He found he could make good money by selling children to work in factories or other places. I remember seeing this man when I returned to Taiwan years later to find my family. He looked at me as if he saw a ghost and ran from me. The whole time I was there I was told, "That man, the one who sold you, is very afraid of what you might do to him. He will not show you his face again." If the law on his crimes had not run out at that time, his fears would be very real. I was ready for him!

My father was so very desperate for money. He was also a very angry man. He blamed my mom for all the bad luck and troubles he had encountered. Yes, I was his flesh and blood, just like the rest of his daughters, but I guess he blamed us, too, for the way things had turned out. After talking to his friend, he found a way to pay his debts and have enough money to live on—at least for a little while.

"Let's go…" my dad commanded me one morning. "Get in the car." A beat-up looking sedan sat parked down below our house, on the side of the road. "Come on, I said, let's go!" he insisted. My mother gave me a nod that I was to hurry and obey my father. I ran down the mountain and skidded to a stop in front of the open back door of the car. I was scared, but I got into the backseat.

My dad and 'this man' drove us to the city and around all that day, from factory to factory. "We can try these places first," he told my dad. We'd stop and go inside, my dad trying to convince the owner about what things I could do. But the reply was always the same, "She is too little."

Place after place we tried, and it was always the same response, "She is too little." So, the man finally drove us back to the village. "I'll let you know what I hear. I have to check on a few more places…" his voice trailed off. He said goodbye to my dad and sped off.

It was maybe a day or two later when my dad's friend came back to our house.

"I found this lady who just came back from the United States. Most of her grown children lived there, her son's kids, too. They bought a home there. Her daughter just got divorced and remarried an American. They have money. Lots of money. This lady called me and said she could use a helper for around the house and can pay good money." He explained with a grin, "Sound good?"

I can't really remember the details or much about the circumstances of when I was sold to The Old Lady as her slave. It hadn't occurred to me that all that driving from factory to factory in the days before was to sell me to them. I remember my father telling me that there was this old woman who needed help to clean and cook and that I was going there to help her for a while. I remember the long drive but had no idea where I was going.

Sold

We arrived in Taipei. Such a big city! We drove down a small street and got out of the car. "Come with me," my father commanded, as we walked towards the door of a tall building. His 'friend' knocked on the door. When it opened, we climbed the stairs and entered into an apartment. It was there I saw her for the first time.

The Old Lady had white hair that was combed into a tight bun in back. I knew she was old, but her skin looked soft and supple, much younger than a person her age. She was so clean and neat looking and her clothes were beautiful. The house looked and smelled new and it was much more modern than any in our village. There was a bathroom and many other separate rooms, and lots of furniture. While my father talked, The Old Lady kept a serious face as she listened to him and his broker friend. To me, she was just an old woman in need of a helping hand around the house. I could see the disappointment on her face as she saw my size and how young I was. I never thought of myself as being too little to really do much of anything. I was always doing chores at home, and we all worked hard to do the work we needed to do, no matter how big or small we were. I liked being helpful. I was very good at watching how something was done and then being able to do it perfectly.

But The Old Lady thought I was useless. "She is too little to help me," She complained to my dad. "I'll have to give her a bath, and take care of *her*!" "No, no…" he insisted, "At home she can do a lot of things. She can do all the chores needed around the house." But The Old Lady still seemed uncertain. "Watch," he pulled me towards him, "She knows how to sweep the floor." My dad looked around as The Old Lady quickly grabbed a broom and gave it to me. I swept the whole living room. Back and forth I pushed that broom, which was just as tall as I was, until the floor was swept clean. The Old Lady would later tell me, "I tested you and you passed the test. That is why I let you come stay with me. But nobody else wants you. If it wasn't for me, nobody would want you."

The Contract

"You must stay here for a while, helping The Old Lady." My father said, as he headed towards the door. "She is like a grandma to you." Then he turned to The Old Lady and his friend as some final words were spoken, and they left. The door closed as I stood there staring at it and at The Old Lady's back as I heard her lock the door. My heart was pounding.

"Well?" The Old Lady said as she turned around to face me. "What else can you do?"

I stood staring at The Old Lady, trying to make sense of what was happening. My parents had sold me to be a slave to this woman, but I had known nothing about any of this. A contract was given to my parents. I had no idea for how long or for how much. My life was drastically altered at that moment and it would take years for me to fully understand it all. I was put to work right then serving this Old Lady in whatever she wanted me to do. Her words began harsh from this first day on and she would constantly remind me of who I was, *her slave.*

Chapter 5

My New 'Family'

The narrow street was filled with dreary dark buildings that towered above me. The Old Lady's son had owned one that was several stories high, which stood across from several less than reputable businesses. The Old Lady, and of course now me, lived on the first floor of this building by ourselves while her son and his girlfriend, lived on another. Other floors were rented out to various tenants and the top floor was mostly storage for The Old Lady's son's business. "You must help 'grandma' with whatever she needs you to do," were my father's last words to me. I pulled the window curtain closed as the Old Lady had told me to, for it was late and my chores for her had not yet been completed. I would have to rub her legs and pat her hand late into the night, a routine that would continue until the day I left her. Those in search of a drink or two visited the bars across the street that were squeezed in between the buildings that housed people and the questionable 'nightlife'; not a scene that a small girl should see out the window. I counted down the days, hoping each would be my last here for my mom had assured me when I left with my father, "In ten days I will come and bring you home. You know how to count, Lunlun? Ten days." My mother had promised. "She will come back for me," I whispered to myself as I blocked out the drunken voices, calling to one another outside. I closed my eyes. "She promised me she will come back for me."

Get to Work

"Make some rice," the Old Lady barked at me, all the while mumbling loudly under her breath how small and useless I was and how she would have to watch everything I did around her house. My days would begin early, before the sun would rise and she made sure the work was non-stop. As I prepared the rice my thoughts went back to the day my mother had taught me how to make rice for the first time. I had been making rice since I was old enough to hold a pot. I carefully filled the pot with water. It was heavy and I was so very small, but I did it. Too small to reach the stove, I pushed a small stool close enough to be able to stand on and continued my task. I was a very fast learner—tell me, show me just once—and I could do it. Whatever the chore might be I worked hard to please the grandma, all the while longing for my mother to come and get me and take me back home.

Weeks passed, and it became difficult to hide my sadness from the grandma. "What is wrong with you?" She prodded one day. "I don't want to look at this sad face anymore! It makes you slow in your work." Holding back the tears, I began to complain that weeks had now passed without any sign of my mother returning for me. "My father told me Mama would come for me—she promised." I choked, my throat painfully tight, for it was all I could do without bursting out crying. "Your mother is never coming for you!" the grandma fired back, her words nearly slapping me across the face with their impact. "I paid good money for you—not that you were worth what I gave that man; you are so small. Why I paid so much, I don't know! If you want to go back there you must pay me what I paid him!" The Old Lady demanded, "Your parents sold you for $10,000 NTD.[1] From now on you will stay here. You will never go back home again!"

So that was it. I had been sold. I was only seven years old, but I knew what that meant. My family had truly sold me as a servant, a slave to this—this bitter and angry old lady, my 'grandma' as I was to call her. My heart sank deep inside me like a stone. And now the real person I was—the strong, confident fighter—curled up from this betrayal, and I just zipped her up inside like a jacket. How does a seven-year-old little girl understand all this? I had to have love, acceptance, a family. And although this grandma of mine would never treat me as family, I tried to do all I could to get that love and acceptance from her. I kept that tenacious, outspoken fighter locked up and silent and I, Little Lunlun, disappeared and the slave, Hsiao-feng, was born.

---

1   that is about $310.00 U.S. dollars

Life with 'Grandma'

"How many times must I tell you to get up and make my breakfast!" The Old Lady barked, the way she always talked to me. She had a way with every word she said of making me feel stupid, incompetent, and worthless. I carried those words on my shoulders like a beast of burden, nearly hunched over from the weight of them. She kicked the mat I laid on and I jumped to my feet. It was nearly 5 a.m. and one of the first times I had ever overslept. My routine was to be up before five to make The Old Lady her breakfast, lay out her clothes for the day and begin my chores for the household, which included cleaning the floor we lived on, the second floor that had an office where the son conducted his business, and all of the rooms in this large building. My days were long and every minute not cleaning was spent attending to The Old Lady's needs. I was up before dawn and rarely went to bed before midnight. I was not given a bed at all to sleep in, but a mat was laid on the floor in the Old Lady's bedroom and only on truly cold nights was I given a shabby, old blanket to keep warm. I had no pillow, but found some smelly old rags that I managed to fashion a sort of pillow out of for myself. The smell of them both made me sick. As I jumped to my feet, I clumsily made my way into the kitchen and prepared her first meal. Of course I was never allowed to sit at the table and eat with The Old Lady nor was I allowed to cook for myself but waited for her to finish, cleaned up her dishes and then took whatever leftovers that were there, and squatted in the corner to eat my 'breakfast'. I was truly a slave in every sense of the word—nothing to call my own and no comforts in life to speak of. The Old Lady would never see me as family, although for the sake of outsiders she called me 'granddaughter.' She barely saw me as human, not an ounce of pity would she spare towards me and not a penny would she spend on me as well. I was not allowed to eat out of a bowl *she* might use, nor use a pair of her chopsticks. I had one bowl and one spoon I would use all of my life with her and sometimes, only my hands to eat with. "You are a slave," she would remind me almost daily. "You cannot use the same dishes I use. You cannot eat at the same table as me. You are not, and will never, ever be equal to me!"

Life became so very hard living with my 'grandma.' She was a cruel and demanding woman who was angry all the time. I was small and tried my best to do everything she wanted. At first, I broke a lot of dishes because I was too little to reach into the cupboards. The Old Lady would slap my face when I broke things. No matter how hard I tried to do right for her she was not satisfied. She was old then, and her mind was made up that I was not good enough and I was not going to change that. She would never be pleased with me.

Stylish Old Lady

In spite of lacking in compassion, The Old Lady did not lack in taste—especially for fine clothing. She was a woman of wealth. Her son owned properties, as well as her daughter, and although her husband had died years ago, he must've left her plenty of money to live on. All of her clothes were handmade for her in China of the finest silks. The colors were brilliant and all the fine details of birds and designs were hand stitched with care. Every day I laid out her clothes, making sure they matched perfectly. She had light weighted silks for summer to keep her cool in the humid Taipei days, and thicker insulated outfits for winter when the weather turned much colder. Reds and yellows, turquoise and greens—this task I grew quite good at and it wouldn't be long before my accomplishment received a nod (but of course with a smirk) rather than the usually berating. I believe it was this chore that developed the talent (and the taste) for fine fashion in me. I just knew what would look good together and how to construct her outfits. In the drudgery of every day, I could, for just a moment, pretend I was someone else, living somewhere else, far away from my life.

Living in Taipei was so different than living in my village. Even though the house was better—she had electricity and an indoor toilet—I didn't want to live here with her; I still wanted to go home. Life in the big city could've been exciting—if I were ever allowed outside of the apartment walls of The Old Lady's home. The Old Lady did not lack for anything. I, on the other hand, lived like the poorest street child. I had come to live with The Old Lady with just the clothes on my back, but even a tiny little girl eventually grows, and soon my clothes and shoes did not fit. I would not be treated as a true 'grandchild', but was ignored. And so were my needs for clothes and shoes and school. The Old Lady would blame me for the way I looked, knowing it was her responsibility. I learned quickly to wash out my own clothes each night if I wanted them clean and to pay attention to even the smallest details, so I would not be beat or yelled at for doing something wrong.

Abuse Begins

My days with The Old Lady were so tiring. I remember her telling me what chores I would do and how to bathe her and wrap her legs. She had so many beauty treatments to keep her skin looking smooth and soft—and it was! She looked so young! I swear, I never did see a wrinkle on her face at all. But for such a little girl as me to serve her needs, be with her every second of the day…I couldn't keep up at first. I remember the first time I was helping her bathe. I'd scrub her back and help her in and out of the tub. She wouldn't go to sleep until I massaged her legs. It was so late at night, yet she insisted I massage her feet as she fell asleep. So I did. I rubbed and rubbed them but before I knew it I, too, had fallen asleep. I always sat on the floor. I was never allowed to sit on a couch or chair or on her bed. Funny, I remember her room had this red carpeting on the floor. I had to reach up as I massaged her feet. Well, when I fell asleep, I somehow peed myself. She must've woken up and saw that I was asleep and then noticed the wet spot all around me. That's when she had a fit!

"You *will* clean your mess up spotlessly or you will have to lick your pee off the rug!" she screamed. "Did you hear what I said?! You will clean this up, NOW, or lick that pee up off my carpet!" She was ranting and raving and acting like a crazy person. I cried and cried and finally said, "I am so sorry, Grandma, so sorry. Don't be mad. I will clean it. I will clean it." I quickly found some rags and began cleaning it. "You are an animal! How come you peed the floor like an animal?!" she continued her tirade, "Clean this up, NOW!" I was so tired, it was after midnight, but I cleaned it. I cried all the while, but I cleaned it up.

My Hair

"Sit still!" she demanded, as she grabbed my ear, pulling my head and neck to the left as she hacked at my hair with a pair of scissors. I watched the soft dark clumps fall to the ground, a few stray strands landing on my thigh and with the jerk of my head from The Old Lady's harsh grasp, fell upon my toes. I sat still, angry, holding back my frustrated tears. The Old Lady forced me to have my hair cut this way. She didn't want me to look like a girl. She cut it so short. I didn't want to see what I looked like when she finished. "Clean this up!" she demanded as she pushed me from the chair, apparently done with me. "Sweep up every bit of it, you lazy girl." I reached my hand behind my neck and felt the bare skin as I brushed the bits of hair away which had begun to make me itch. This was now how my hair would always look from now on. Short. Choppy. Boy-like. Of the only pictures taken of me when I was a child that would exist, these would be the ones. And pictures were taken. I think now they were done to prove that I was just a happy 'granddaughter', not the unhappy slave girl, separated from her real family. I looked happy in most of those pictures. The clothes I wore in them were cleaner, better ones. They tried to show I was happy; how could I be a slave? I was smiling, but I had to. I did like to smile—it lights up my whole face. You can see this whenever I smile. I remember this one picture sent by The Old Lady to my sisters, me in a red sweater. I saw that picture years later on the news. I felt angry inside when I saw it knowing how I felt then. It was all such a lie. As I grew older, the pictures started to show the despair inside me more and more. There was a picture taken of me when I was about 10 years old. My smile is missing. You can see the light inside me had grown so very dim at that time.

I look back and think, "There was something very wrong with that Old Lady." At times her behavior towards me was so horrid and bizarre. But through this all I still had love for her, even when I hated her. She was the only family I knew.

No Comfort

Day after horrible day, I'd get up and work—clean, cook, be at The Old Lady's demand. I'd think about my mom and dad and what they did. Sometimes I'd cry and miss them so much. Every day was miserable. There were days, though, The Old Lady might show me some kindness, when she saw how sad I was. She would offer maybe five minutes of comfort saying, "Come here, it will be alright. You are ok." She was actually nice to me! Those were good days. I would think, "Oh my god, today is a good day; she is nice to me today; maybe things will be okay." When I was little this was easier to take. It was easier to smile, but I wasn't really happy. It wasn't real.

On bad days, I'd be so angry. "I wish they all could be punished!" I'd think. "My mom and dad and this grandma, they deserve to feel how I feel for what they all have done to me!" I'd even be mad at God sometimes. "Why did You let them do this to me? Why do You let this Old Lady treat me the way she does?" I could feel hate just boil inside of me. I would imagine all kinds of terrible punishments to justify how I was treated, but when I gave in to this bitter anger my days dragged on in hopelessness. It was a huge weight on my shoulders, pressing down on me—heavier and heavier—until I couldn't bear it anymore. "Do you feel what the hate is doing to you?" It was as if God was saying this to me. "Can you carry this day after day and live?" And I would carry that hate and then lay it down for a while and feel some relief, but it was always there, baiting me to pick it back up again. I would think of my mother's words, "Tomorrow will be better." I would say that over and over to myself. I was on the edge of tears almost every day. "Okay, I have no mother now, but will this grandma finally care about me?"

School

I remember looking out the window of that apartment, high up over the street, overlooking the older concrete or 'no style' buildings here or there, much like the one I lived in, watching the young people hurrying to school. I wanted to go, too, and often asked The Old Lady, "Why don't I go to school?" Her answer was always the same, that I was too stupid, that school would do no good to someone like me… and so on. My heart would ache and I watched those children, wearing their new school clothes, carrying their backpacks of books and chasing each other as they went down the street.

There was a time when uniformed men came to the door to check if we were supposed to live in this building—we had to show paperwork—proving we were not illegal citizens, as many people would hire undocumented workers. "Why is she not in school?" One of the officers said, pointing to me. I looked at The Old Lady and she lied saying, "She is my grand-daughter. Her father has not changed the paperwork for her to go to school here yet.

Once, when The Old Lady made a trip to visit her daughter, I was to stay in Taipei. We were living in a different building I think then. The Old Lady had a sister who lived a few doors down and she was to care for me while The Old Lady was gone. This woman had been a school teacher. She was much more understanding than her sister and took some pity on me, bringing some books and teaching supplies to me to give me a few lessons. I remember this little book; it had letters and picture in it. I had never been to school or watched any TV or movies, so I had not been exposed to any education other than the street signs I had seen out the window or on the way to church or market with The Old Lady. I was grateful for this opportunity, as short as it was, but when The Old Lady returned and discovered what her sister had begun, an argument broke out between them and I was never to be looked after by her sister again. I faintly remember hearing her sister say, "She must have lessons! It isn't right to keep her from school. I can teach her if you don't send her for studies." The Old Lady could be completely unreasonable and dismissive. If she felt that something should not be, then it would not be. The Old Lady always won out and so I never went to school nor received another lesson again after that.

Always Hungry

The Old Lady was so unstable and unpredictable at times. She would get something in her head—mostly a suspicion about what I was up to—and I would get punished. She was obsessed with me stealing her food. I was never allowed to eat anything but her scraps and leftovers, but that was still too good for a 'slave' like me. If I opened the cupboards, she would say, "You cannot just open my cupboards without asking," I thought, "Why can't I if I am her granddaughter?" She would get angry and say, "You know why I hate you? Because you do something wrong though I am trying to teach you." I would obey her because I was little and accepted what she said as right, after all, she took me in when my family had chosen to sell me.

Stealing Bread

I was always thinking about food because I was always hungry. Once we had gone to the store and I saw some bread.

It looked so good! I looked around to see if The Old Lady was watching and then I stole it. I tried to hide it. We always went hiking and I carried The Old Lady's backpack. On our way back from the hike we had stopped at the store, so I put the bread in that bag. I didn't know that the cashier had seen me do this. I was SO hungry. She told The Old Lady, "This little girl stole this bread." The Old Lady apologized to the cashier, but when we got home she began hitting me and pulling my hair.

"How dare you do this after all I have done for you!" she ranted. "You are a thief and I will teach you not to steal and embarrass me!" She grabbed her cane and began beating me with it until red welts shown all over my legs. I cried out in pain saying, "No…no, I promise. I won't do it again, please, Grandma, no, no!" She grabbed my hair and pulled me to the ground, yanking my head and twisting my neck, screaming the whole time, "You thief!" I couldn't fight her for the pain would only be worse. I just lay there like a cloth doll. When she had finished her violent outburst, she pushed my head down and walked away. I sat in a heap, crying, my legs throbbing where her bamboo cane had stung me with its sharp quick blows. I rubbed them as the swollen red marks appeared leaving pinkish red stripes up and down my legs. I cried and cried wishing I could run someplace and hid but there was nowhere. The tears rolled down my cheek silently for I knew if The Old Lady heard me I might get another beating. I got up and went to the bathroom and found a rag. I only knew to put some cold water on each place I was hit so the swelling would go down.

I did this quickly because she'd coming looking for me and would not be pleased if I didn't return to my chores.

I could not go to the store with her from that moment on without her embarrassing me, watching me, making a fool of me by saying to everyone who worked there, "I am watching her; this thief won't do anything." She did this every time. I was so humiliated. I never stole again.

Soured Food

I never got enough to eat so I was very skinny.

The Old Lady was a good cook and although I helped cook, she prepared the main dishes while I watched to learn how. We ate traditional foods like pig leg—for a special occasion, or Chinese New Year. She loved to cook chicken. I once opened her refrigerator and saw all of the food The Old Lady had in there. Every shelf and drawer was filled! She was just one person, and her son, of course, but there was so much food! I couldn't help saying, "Wow!" when I saw this. I was tempted, and this is the only time this happened, but I took something and ate it. I don't remember what it was, but I do remember shoving it into my mouth. I was so hungry! I was always so hungry. After she found out—and she always found things out—she started counting everything…everything she cooked. If she made some chicken, she counted how many she ate, how many were left. As food cooks it shrinks down. She would look in the pot and say, "Did you take some? Why is this piece so small? You cut some off and ate it. I see you looking at my food, you jealous thief!"

One day she began screaming at me this way, "You steal my food! This is how you repay me? I know you took my food!" "Grandma, I did not take your food. I would not do that!" I said, but she didn't believe it, so she slapped me across the face. "My food is too good for you. From now on you will eat only what is spoiled, and NOT my leftovers. They are much too good for you!"

Whatever had soured or had gone bad, she would tell me to eat that. What could I do? I was so hungry I had to eat it. This continued for quite a while, until slowly she changed her mind and I got more leftovers once again, but she would always put her chewed bones or discarded food on top of the food I ate. I would pull off the half-eaten pieces and pick what I could off for myself. I don't like pork to this day and I think this is why, always the tough fatty pieces that she had chewed on were left for me.

The Lock

When dinner or any meal was eaten, The Old Lady—and her son and his girlfriend if they were there—ate at the table. I stood up to eat or sat on the floor. Once when her daughter was visiting and saw that I was eating on the floor she asked about it. "Mom, why does she eat on the floor like that?" The Daughter asked. The Old Lady answered, "She is dirty…a slave…she cannot use the same chopsticks as we do. She cannot sit with us." I would wait until I was allowed to eat. The food would have a sour smell or bits of mold on the corners, but I had to eat it. I was hungry. I never ever ate enough to feel full.

I remember once she had made sticky rice cakes. She'd always make ten or six or five or eight of something, never four. Numbers mean something in our culture. It'd mean bad luck to make four, especially for the New Year. Bad luck all year! On this day when she counted, somehow one was missing. "You took that rice cake, I know you did, you worthless slave!" She became furious! "You want my sticky rice? You can't control your lust for it?" She grabbed me around the neck and shoved a ball of the rice into my face, forcing it into my lips. I choked in her tight grip as bits of the sticky grains smeared over my face, went up my nose and lodged between my gums. "That is the last time you will have my sticky rice!" she growled. She stomped out of the room. I sat on the floor picking out the pieces of rice that were stuck everywhere. I wiped the tears away as I saw her storm back into the room with a small chain and lock and place it through the handles on the refrigerator. When she stepped back, the refrigerator was locked up tight so I could not get into it! Can you imagine that! If I needed to cook or be in the kitchen for any reason, The Old Lady would watch me like a hawk.

The Toothache

I never ate sweets—only once a year, at Chinese New Year. There would be a box of candy and I would get one piece. It's funny, I have had only one cavity in my whole life. One day my tooth suddenly started hurting really bad. I had gotten up that morning and felt this dull pain that got worse as the day went on. When I couldn't hide it any longer, I began crying. I was crying and crying. I tried to tell The Old Lady what I felt, but of course she would not listen. "Grandma, something is not right with my tooth. There is a lot of pain and it will not stop." This went on for several months. The Old Lady grew tired at times of my suffering, but her solution was to slap me. "This is your fault! I am nice enough to give you one treat and this is how you repay me?! I am sure you stole more candies when I was not aware of it. You deserve the pain!"

My face grew swollen over time and it became hard to hide. Six months had passed when The Old Lady's sister noticed something was very wrong. "You must take her to the doctor!" she told her sister. I could see the anger in The Old Lady's eyes when her sister scolded her for waiting so long. She took me to the dentist, begrudgingly, threating that I must pay her back every penny. I guess I was very lucky, although I had to have the tooth removed surgically, because it was so badly infected, I was otherwise ok. It's funny because a new tooth grew in its place! When I was very little I remember some of my teeth were loose and falling out and my dad would pull them out and say, "If you don't, you will not get double," People see me now and look at my teeth and comment how nice they look. "How come you are getting younger, not older?" they say.

Chapter 6

The Routine

Walking was a daily routine with the Old Lady, she was religious about it. Not a day went by without me trudging besides her, her arm leaning heavily upon my shoulder, her umbrella in hand, more for hitting and poking me with than shielding her from tropical rains. She was always impeccably dressed, in winter, in her ornately detailed, hand-stitched long coat or in summer, in her delicate pastel pants and beautifully embroidered silk jacket, flapping in the breeze as we walked on and on. She had this way of carrying herself, a slow, almost parade march, as if she were someone of importance. I admired that at times, wishing for her approval, which I would never receive. She was always smartly dressed, whatever the season or activity, with no exception. We'd get up by 5 a.m. to begin the day. I don't think The Old Lady ever slept in a day in her life. Sometimes I'd daydream of just sleeping until the sun woke up before me, shining its light and warmth over my face, soaking it all in until I'd had enough.

I felt tired. I was always tired. Even as a young child, I felt exhausted all the time. I guess I should be grateful for these outings; at least I could get outdoors and be distracted from the grueling household chores I had to do. I was not out on my own, but still, I would be out where there were sights and sounds and besides, whenever there were people around, The Old Lady was not as cruel to me; she'd never outright hit me in public, other than the constant brutal jabs from her umbrella or cruel pinching of my arms.

This is how we always walked about. To most who saw us passing by, it might have seemed endearing, a grandmother with her grandchild helping her with shopping and such. Whether they knew my plight and turned a blind eye to it, or whether they were completely oblivious to what life I was trapped in, no one said a word. I called her Grandma, so why would they question her?

We had a purpose in where we were going each day and a set way in which to do it. We trekked daily to a natural mineral hot springs spa called Yang Ming Shan. We would have to walk several blocks, then catch a bus and take the long ride up the hillside towards the springs. I dreaded this. Though The Old Lady was dressed beautifully, I was always in the same clothes, stained from doing chores in them and usually thread bare. I would have to wash all of my clothes by hand and hang them to dry each night, and in the humid Taipei air I couldn't be sure they'd always dry in time, so I wore them many times before I washed them, so they smelled. I was very conscience of this as we traveled about—I looked every bit of the slave I felt like inside.

The Bus

The bus ride was a very long one. Sometimes I had to stand, if the bus was quite full. The Old Lady never put me on her lap, nor let me take a seat if she felt someone else deserved to sit other than me. When I sat, I longed to fall asleep, but if The Old Lady saw me with my eyes closed, a sharp poke from her umbrella would bring me back to my unfortunate reality.

I got so hungry on those long rides up the mountain. I rarely ate any breakfast before we went out, maybe a leftover scrap of bread, if I was lucky. Trying my best not to let The Old Lady see me, I would look for left-over food on the bus. The bus would go to the end of its stop before it turned around and headed back up. The driver made everyone get off the bus as it did this. Sometimes people would leave their half-eaten food on a seat, or if I was lucky a piece of fruit at the bottom of a bag on the ground. One day someone must've forgotten their lunch. I saw this bag carefully folded at the top just sitting by itself on a seat towards the back. I hurriedly walked towards it, blocking its view from The Old Lady. I put the backpack I carried in front of me and then set it in front of the lunch bag. Unzipping the pack and as quick as I could, I shoved the lunch bag into the back of my bag and closed it. The bus took off. Carefully, when The Old Lady wasn't looking, I stole bits of it, as quietly as I could, as the bus rocked and bumped its way back towards the mountain.

When we reached the top we still had to walk quite a ways, all steep uphill. Trees lined either side of the road as it twisted upward, getting ever more narrow as it climbed towards the springs. I remember we'd stop at a parklike nature area for a while. Here, many old people sat, sitting upon benches made from large rocks, whose tops had been polished to a shiny flat seat of blues and greens. Tables were made the same way, but resemble more of a real table, round with a pedestal of reddish gray rock underneath. Flowers and moss-covered trees and railings making the little park look cold even on a sunny day.

Then that *smell* would meet my nose—the strong sulfur from the natural mineral rich waters which flowed like a little river through the entire area. Sturdy stone bridges kept the path moving across the rushing stream and small pools bubbled with the bright cloudy water as we walked the path towards the baths. I remember seeing this little tree, not much taller than me, which was trimmed to look like an umbrella. Here we would stop and rest a moment. My mind would often get lost as I watched the people who passed by. The Old Lady often met and talked with her acquaintances who sat and rested after a day of bathing in the mineral springs. I would stand by her side in silence, not allowed to move or do anything until she was finished visiting. God forbid I had to go to the restroom, which would happen from time to time. This would infuriate her as it interrupted her social time. She wouldn't let me go by myself or be out of her sight for one moment. She would have to walk with me, and angrily let me know by a poke of her cane, here and there, that I was not pleasing to her by doing this.

Private Bath

I don't know if The Old Lady paid to rent a small bath and dressing area in the spa area, but I know this small room was 'hers' with no doubt. We would go into this building at the top of the mountain and then into the small private bath area. I'd then help her to undress and change into a bathing suit so she could sit in the healing mineral waters. I truly believe these waters did have a healing effect upon her for she was an old woman and yet her skin was young and soft, and glowed. She was a beautiful old lady and taking care of herself in this way kept her looking young well into her nineties.

The Old Lady would spend several hours in the private baths before she'd had enough, and then I would help to dry her off and get her dressed again. "Be careful with my clothes, you stupid girl! They are never to be folded or creased," she'd scold. "You are so useless! If I hadn't taken you in, no one would have!" And I would mumble, "Yes, Grandma," politely, hoping to avoid a possible slap that might come my way. She really had such beautiful clothes and I did admire and respect the care that went into making them. I did learn much about style and color and quality from dressing The Old Lady, and I have to admit, I got quite good at pairing her outfits together.

The Waiting

When I finished dressing her and gathering her belongings, we headed back towards the park to sit and perhaps visit some more. I hated the waiting. Waiting for The Old Lady to finish talking; waiting for The Old Lady to finish bathing; waiting for The Old Lady to finished whatever she did. Waiting, waiting, waiting. I would stand and wait. I guess this might seem crazy, I mean, it was a break from sweeping or cleaning or washing, but at least my mind was free to think when I was doing those things. I couldn't be free to think while waiting. I had to anticipate her need. If she thought for a minute I wasn't be attentive—slap, hit, pinch, poke! I never felt more like a slave that standing there—waiting to perform my next act of service!

Finally, The Old Lady would grow hungry and we would walk down a path towards this vendor who owned a more permanent stand and eat lunch. I loved the smell of the sticky rice he steamed in little folded packets wrapped in bamboo leaves. The Old Lady would order her meal and I would again wait, this time hoping she wouldn't be so hungry as to eat all of what was on her plate that I might have enough of the leftovers to fill my hungry stomach as well.

I hated it when she would order fish! That meant that she would plop the chewed head or tail on top of her leftovers for me. I'd have to pick whatever pieces I could off the mangled discards and sift through the tiny bones that fell into the clumps of rice.

I can still smell the heavenly scented food freshly pre-pared by vendors with their carts as we traveled back towards the bus; the smell of stinky tofu, my favorite, as well as various meats on skewers and every type of steamed noodle imagin-able. My stomach grumbled in vain as we continued on, for I knew we wouldn't be stopping to eat anything else. I carried a bag, which held some fruit and other items The Old Lady would snack on, if she felt hungry, on our long journey home.

Sadness Sets in

It's funny how difficult times color the memories we hold. It's so hard to remember those years in Taipei. I was there but wasn't there. I should have fond memories of things such as the Botanical Gardens in the summer time, the heady fruity-sweet scent of the Lotus flowers blooming, the Japanese white-eyed birds darting through the trees, or the red brick walls in the historic block, or the fragrant incense at Longshan Temple or the sights and sounds of the night market, walking through the noisy crowded street, those selling their wares calling to the shoppers. I never stopped nor was allowed to stop and buy anything of my own.

For those who have never been to a market place in Tai-wan, you have missed such a feast of the senses! The streets are like a beehive, humming with activity. Every corner, ev-ery crevice is alive with things to see, smell and taste. During the morning, wonderful smells of cooking come from every-where—delicious scents of soups and noodles, pastries and meats. If you weren't hungry before you began your shopping, you soon would be in a matter of moments. Once when The Old Lady and I were shopping, she was looking for something down one of the streets, I saw a man, deep into a back corner of his shop, which was no wider than a few feet across, covered in what looked like dust. This dust covered everything! I saw him roll out a huge bolt of something and he poured more 'dust' on it and then with a large knife, cut it into strips. When he gathered up the strips, I saw that they were noodles! The dust was flour he had sprinkled over the dough before rolling, folding and cutting it out. I was amazed! My eyes took this all in as fast as I could, for we were not there to sightsee. Carrots, onions, greens of all kinds, papaya, pineapple, mango, and Sakya (or sugar apple) were on table after table. Displays of mushrooms and shellfish and things of all kinds were in boxes, on long tables or on carts. Butchers set up their stands, cutting meats to size, and everywhere you looked, something new and different. But the smells! Those delicious smells! Sticky rice and stinky tofu! The longer we walked these streets, the more my stomach growled. I knew The Old Lady would buy and eat tasty things such as these but I would be lucky only to eat her scraps; and what places we'd visit was at her mercy—hurrying to church and then home; accompanying her on her daily walk and then home; dutifully grocery shop and then home; waiting on her hand and foot at the spa and then home. The things that make life exciting and adventurous, full of color and pictures and smells were held back from me. I should have those memories, yet in my mind the memories are all gray and colorless.

A writer once wrote, "Taipei has a color like the sun and the source of this color is the good days enjoyed there, a cherished childhood and brilliant golden memories."[1] I wish it had been so for me. Sadness set in. Days had become filled with heartache. My mother had told me there were to be bad days, but tomorrow had hope. I hoped now, that what she said was true.

Taipei was growing rapidly in the 1980s. Wide tree lined boulevards were added along with newer apartment blocks, more stylish than our own, and more upscale restaurants and cafes sprung up around the booming city. I was growing too, mostly out of my clothes once again, but as I approached my teen years something unusual happened.

Changes

"Oh, my gosh…" I whispered to myself. I saw a stream of blood running down my leg. I was sweeping the floor at the time, so I went to the bathroom and shut the door behind me. The shorts I wore felt wet near the crotch and as I looked closer, I saw that it was blood. I had started my period and had no idea what was going on. No one ever told me anything about *anything*, certainly not about having monthly menstruation. I never saw TV or movies, I could not read a book—I had no idea when this first happened what in the world was going on. Could I be really sick? What did I do to myself?!

---

1   Wang Zhen-xu

When The Old Lady found out she said, "You did something bad! You filthy thing!" She was furious! She got so mad she began to hit me. I pulled my hands up over my head as she struck me again and again. She did not explain what was happening to me, after her attack was done, she just walked away, screaming at me to clean myself up. She never gave me pads. I had to use toilet paper. In Taiwan, we don't have rolls of toilet paper, it is more like a pack of tissues, not at all like in the U.S. I formed a pad out of a stack of tissues, but I didn't have underwear so what could I do? My clothes were always so limited. I never had underwear, never even a bra! Usually, just a few ill-fitting clothes were what I wore until they were too tight or threadbare.

I was so desperate at what to do I ended up using an old grocery bag, trying to fashion some sort of plastic under garment to hold the tissue. Can you believe it?! My chores and life didn't change when my period started, I just had to adapt and deal with it. No supplies or compassion would be extended to me.

Once when The Old Lady and I went on her usual trek to Yang Ming Shan and the hot springs there, behind where she bathed, there was a place which was open to a wooded area so as you enjoyed the mineral baths you could also enjoy a view of nature. I began to throw the old wads of tissue from my makeshift 'pads' out behind the trees, hoping to hide this from The Old Lady. She would never let me out of her site, even forcing me to 'hold it' for long periods of time when I had to use the restroom. When she wasn't looking, sitting in the mineral waters with her back to me, I would throw the blood-soaked tissues as far as I could. It wasn't long before the owners (groundkeepers?) found them and wondered why blood-stained tissues were thrown out there. Of course, it was only a matter of time before The Old Lady would find out and questioned me about it.

"It's you, isn't it?" She confronted me one day. This was such a stressful thing for me to experience each month, not having what I needed to deal with it and not even knowing why this was happening to me that I blurted out to her in my frustration, my voice filled with sharp angry tones, "Of course, it's me! What can I do? You don't give me anything—not even underwear to wear—for *this*! What am I to do? If I don't use anything, you're mad at me; I *use* something you're mad at me." I continued like this for a minute or two completely forgetting about the tone I used or what might happen to me. I think I got away with this because The Old Lady did not like to be embarrassed in front of anyone or that someone would hear or know about her business. I was pretty loud when I said this to her. Thank God, it was finally some of her neighbors who had wondered why I always wore the same clothes and one day asked her about me. They even asked if I had begun my period. It was these generous neighbors who donated pads and some underwear to me. God was so good!

It was so confusing to me when I would get my period. "Why does it come back, and sometimes it doesn't?" I would ask myself. I can't remember how I finally figured it out. The

Old Lady felt ashamed that the neighbors had noticed this, so she began buying the pads regularly.

As I got older, I began to get a little bolder to ask her for clothes, mostly near Chinese New Year. This was the only time The Old Lady would give me anything.

My Clothes

The bulk of my clothes were always donations. Donations were given to The Old Lady by church members or neighbors. Some of the donated clothes looked funny. I remember once wearing a set of clothes—they were bright red and green. I looked so weird at times. A neighbor who made clothes gave a lot to me once, they were so big! Some I altered or mended myself. Clothes never fit me right.

I was never allowed to use The Old Lady's washer—so all my clothes and blanket smelled. When I could, I'd wash my clothes out by hand and hope they would dry overnight so they could be worn the next day.

I got shoes maybe once a year. The Old Lady would buy me shoes, but they were so cheap they had to be glued because they'd fall apart after I wore them once or twice. I got hand me down socks from her granddaughter, but they had holes in them. I'd try to hide the holes when I wore them by twisting them to the side or bottom of my foot. I remember this very nice couple from church. The Old Lady had been invited to visit them to have lunch. We walked to their house and knocked on the door. "Come in, come in..." they said. The Old Lady took off her beautiful expensive handmade shoes and set them near the door. I had to take off my shoes, too. I felt so ashamed. I placed my shoes at the door and walked in with The Old Lady leaning on my arm. I was so conscience of my socks with the huge holes in them. This happened often, as The Old Lady frequently attended Bible studies at this house. I'd just fold my socks down, hoping to hide the holes.

I was always wearing the same clothes, same socks. These bright red tennis shoes were once given to me by her sister, used of course. At another time I got a pair of bright orange ones. The Old Lady just never wanted to buy for me. I never had a bra until after I escaped. I had asked her once about a bra, but she just never wanted me to look like a girl. I was growing, so I never knew my size and I wore things until they were too tight to even put on. God always provided when things got very tough, though. The neighbors were kind enough to donate—but not enough to say anything about my situation to others.

Abuse Continues

I helped that Old Lady do everything! I'd help her bathe, wash her back, her hair—everything. If I forgot to do something or I did anything wrong, she'd hit me or throw something at me. Often she'd say nasty things to me, loudly at times in public, maybe she thought she looked powerful, but nobody would say anything to her. They let her abuse me. I was shy back then. I was very conscious of my body. It was changing and I felt awkward about it.

"Come here, NOW!" She once demanded. I always obeyed, so I walked to her fearfully. She grabbed me, pulling my shirt over my head with one hand and holding my arm with the other, until she tore all of my clothes off. "Why are you hiding your body from me?" She pulled me, naked, towards the bathroom and then pushed me into the shower. I was humiliated! She turned the water on and cold forceful streams hit me in the face as I lay on my back, scrambling to stand up. She threw a rag at me and told me to clean myself and the mess up. Then she just walked away.

She was so controlling in that way. I don't know if it was her plan to always treat me this way or if she was generally just a warped unstable woman. I always felt that I had done something so wrong that she was forever going to remind me of it, and punish me for it, every day of my life.

Whatever went on in her mind, she'd find a way to blame me somehow, someway. I was never allowed to use her shower to bathe myself. When I was allowed to take a bath, I was forced to use her old bath water. I hated this! I wasn't allowed to run any water so when she thought I should take a bath, she'd leave that old used water for me. "Get a bucket and bathe," she'd demand, "You stink and are filthy!" I would have to take a little bucket I had, scoop the dirty water from the tub of her used bath water and carry it to a shower in the back. Of course the water wouldn't still be hot or even warm enough.

It made me feel dirty to clean myself with this used water. At other times I would use a rag to take a kind of sponge bath. But I would never let her see me do this. I was at least somewhat grateful that she was a very picky and clean old woman. She took several baths a day

The Daughter

The Old Lady had a daughter who had moved to the United States. She was very much like her mother. She could be just as hurtful and cruel, but she was smart enough to beat me only with her words, never with her hands. She was loyal to whatever her mother decided about any matter, including when it came to me. The Daughter would visit from time to time and at first she seemed to show me some kindness.

Now of course I was never allowed to use clean water—never, ever. And never allowed to use her shampoo or soaps. She was so stingy and cheap with me but not on herself! She had these expensive soaps and shampoos that smelled wonderful. She insisted her daughter mail these toiletries to her from the U.S. She never used shampoo from Taiwan. I had to always help her bathe, but she always kept her eye on me. I had to use the same detergent used to wash the dishes. Once she saw that the color of what I used was the same as the color of one of her fancy shampoos. She had a fit! Flying into a rage, she accused me of taking her precious shampoo from America. "You thief!" she called me. For three days I was yelled at and she told all her friends that I had stolen her shampoo.

"Can you believe what this ungrateful 'granddaughter' of mine did?" She would begin when the ladies from church would come over for tea. I had to stand there, cringing inside, while she went off on how horrible I was. I didn't even do it! Just because the color of the dish soap—green I think it was—was the same as her shampoo. She continued to condemn me long after everyone left, "You are my slave...how can you use my stuff?! You are a slave, you will never be on my same level... you cannot use the same stuff as me...you cannot eat with me!" After that I was forced to use laundry soap, this washing powder, on my body and hair. It was so rough and it irritated my skin and hair. This was so very hurtful for me. I felt so worthless.

Truth and Lies

There are several different religions in Taiwan. My mother believes in God, the Christian God. I was amazed that The Old Lady followed the Christian faith. I would see her reading her Bible and then all of a sudden scream hurtful things at me. Then she would just go back to reading that Holy Book. This was so hard to understand.

Chapter 7

Church

The Old Lady was diligent about attending church. She never missed a service! Of course, I accompanied her everywhere she went so church was no exception.

Every Thursday there was a woman's Bible study. We would walk there—The Old Lady loved to walk! She had a daily routine of walking or hiking which usually started very early in the morning. Carrying her umbrella or cane, she would walk and rest her hand and the heavy weight of her body, on my shoulder. Since the Bible study was from two to four in the afternoon, we would get back to the house just in time for me make dinner.

The church was small and they wore robes on the stage and everyone sang. Half way through the service they would take communion. The Old Lady wouldn't let me participate because I had never been baptized in that church. "You cannot do this with us. You are not a part of this church." She'd say. "You have not been baptized."

The Old Lady was always afraid of anyone getting too close to me. I think she knew that if people talked to me they would find out that I was her slave. The pastor kind of knew something wasn't right with me and the family. But like others in the church, they felt it wasn't any of their business.

Donations

My choice of church clothes was pretty limited. I did have this cream-colored dress, it was long with lace and a red stripe. It was made of a thin material so you could see through it. I had no underwear so I wore shorts underneath it. I wore it every Sunday. People would ask The Old Lady why I wore the same dress over and over again. She'd lie and say, "It's her favorite dress, this is why she always wears it; she won't wear anything else to church." It wasn't true of course; I had nothing else to wear. To keep it clean and from getting worn out, I only wore it to church. Later, I had some grey pants, they were actually black but I bleached them so people would think they were a different pair of pants. She'd then say, "Those are her favorite pants; that is why she always wears them." Others would ask me, "Why do you always wear that all the time? How come you never change your clothes?" So I would take turns with what I had. That was the beginning of people donating clothes to me on a regular basis. One lady from church gave me a sweater. It was so nice of her...it was so soft. I wore it all the time. I was grateful for everything given to me, no matter the color or if it fit me properly.

Loving Church

I truly loved the days we went to church. This is was the place that I could sleep! Because I was always up so late with The Old Lady and working so hard all day, I was exhausted! I also knew she wouldn't dare hit or pinch me in church for fear of what others might think. I felt safe and looked forward to this haven twice a week. In addition to the Thursday Bible study, we attended Sunday services as well. I loved to listen to the messages that were preached! I would carefully sit in such a way as not to look like I was a sleeping but was comfortable enough to drift in and out of slumber, listening to God's Word. I especially loved when the pastor began to read this part about love, it was like the words were meant for me. He read, "Love is patient, love is kind. It does not envy, it does not boast, it is not proud. It does not dishonor others, it is not self-seeking, it is not easily angered, it keeps no record of wrongs. Love does not delight in evil but rejoices with the truth. It always protects, always trusts, always hopes, always perseveres. Love never fails." I thought about these words. "Love is patient, love is kind." That passage is my favorite!

Getting Baptized

The woman behind me in church one day said, "Take one," as she passed communion to me. I knew The Old Lady would not like this. "No, she cannot…" she explained to the woman, interrupting her, "She has not been baptized." It was not too long after this that the pastor met with The Old Lady. He kept pestering her to have me baptized. "God loves her and you come to church all the time, why not let her be baptized? This church is like a family." He said. He told her the next baptism was scheduled for around Christmas time. She finally agreed. She was mad but because of her fear of anyone finding out about me, she let the pastor do this. So that December I was baptized in a pool. I remember how cold the water was! I went down in to the water and The Old Lady just sat there. The service lasted about an hour and they even gave me a certificate. The Old Lady was not happy about it. We didn't continue to attend that church very long after that.

Believing

"Clean out all of this trash." The Old Lady said. "All these useless things from my son's business must be thrown in the trash." She left me in one of the upstairs rooms with a broom and dust bin. I picked up old magazines and catalogues and tossed them in the can. As I was doing this I came across a picture of Jesus. It had been torn out of some book or something and it lay there in the bits of dust and dirt. I carefully picked it up and brushed it off. "I have a place for you," I said to the Savior who had his arms open wide and a heart painted between his robes. My 'bed' at that time was in a little crawlspace where odds and ends were stored. It was only about as wide as my body. I could touch the walls when I lay there. Mice would often run across my chest as I slept at night. I put the picture in my pocket and finished my work. Late that night when I went to lie down, I placed the picture against the wall, fastening it with a piece of tape. "Good night, God," I said. "I know You will help me." This was my altar. I would tell my troubles to Jesus and pray for His help. I believed He hadn't forgotten about me. I believed He would help me.

I remember sharing my story much later on, and I mentioned that The Old Lady followed Christian beliefs, religiously reading her Bible and attended church regularly. So many were shocked; they couldn't understand why she did what she did. How in the world would she treat me in such a way if she was a Christian?

My answer was simple. I told them, "When I went to church with The Old Lady, I listened to God's Words and believed what the pastor said, but The Old Lady—she did not."

Chapter 8

Christmas

"What is THIS?" I thought as I looked at the dark green bushy tufts that were pushing their way out of the long skinny cardboard box that contained them. I had lugged this box and several others of different sizes from where they had been stored away. The Old Lady didn't answer me but just commanded "Put this tree up, over there," motioning towards the corner near the large window that faced the street, with her finger. Her hands as well as the rest of her youthful skin, were so soft and smooth, never revealing her age, just the years of pampering and of being well taken care of by others. "Over…there!" she barked again, this time adding, "Are you deaf, you stupid girl?" spitting her words out, as if they left a bad taste in her mouth.

Hurriedly I unpacked the boxes and began to study this strange new addition to the room. The branches of this 'Christmas Tree' were made of some sturdy material and were heavy. I tugged and pulled until I was able to free this thing from its box. Some branches were long and full while others, short and sparse. There was something about this 'tree' that immediately filled me with joy as I stood it up in place.

I opened the other boxes and found all kinds of decorations; strings of lights and delicate ornaments, each with a small hook. It was like my own treasure chest, overflowing with precious items. The Old Lady left the decorating to me and I got to choose where to hang each one. I had no idea of what this all meant or why I was now dressing a tree that would occupy the corner of the room for several weeks, but I felt a peace come over me that I rarely felt in this house. One by one I hung the ornaments as a tiny toy music box played tunes such as Jingle Bells, over and over again. Strand after strand of lights were tucked onto every branch, colors twinkled in reds, yellows, blues and greens and for an hour or two in my life I no longer felt like a slave, but just another girl in this world.

The Tree

This 'Christmas Tree' became a yearly tradition that I looked forward to with excitement. Some years we had a real tree brought in to the house (for although this was such a foreign holiday in Taiwan, The Old Lady knew how to get what she wanted.) I loved those years! The smell of the fresh tree, and the hours I spent decorating kept me from having to do other chores such as washing clothes by hand or scrubbing the floors—at least until the next day. When the tree was finally filled with its shiny bulbs of gold and silver, The Old Lady would bring out her collection of Christmas music.

Soon the music box tunes changed to cassette tapes of Christmas Carols. There was no fanfare or explaining, "This is what Christmas is all about," Nothing. Just music and decorating. It's funny, but I remember that all of the songs were sung in English. But even though I couldn't understand a word, the voices lifted me far away from my sad life. What was this 'Christmas'? And why did it bring such hope and peace to me? No one needed to explain it for what I felt inside was explanation enough. This was MY holiday, my time to feel like a human being. "O Holy Night…the stars were shining brightly… it is the night of our dear Savior's birth…" I loved this song!

O Holy Night

It was a chilly night, at least for Taiwan. I was glad at least it was not raining. I pulled my jacket up close to my neck. It was worn too thin to really keep out the cold wind as we made our way to church that night. It was Christmas! The thoughts of twinkling lights and echoes of Christmas hymns warmed my heart enough as we stepped into church. It was my own secret holiday, for most Taiwanese did not celebrate Christmas as an official holiday, and what it truly is, the birth of Jesus Christ, the Savior. But for me, it was a time I looked forward to each year. I also looked forward to anytime we spent in church for The Old Lady couldn't scold or hit me there. At church there was to be a potluck because it was Christmas.

"You will sit at my feet and not say a word," The Old Lady instructed. "This potluck will have much food, but you are my slave. You will not sit with me and eat, understood?" We arrived early and the pastor's wife met us at the door. "Welcome, and Happy Christmas!" she said. "Come and sit at the table. We have so much food. Your granddaughter can sit here next to me." She looked at me and smiled. "No…it will be no trouble for her to sit next to me, by my feet on the floor; why have her take up a seat when perhaps someone else who needs to sit can be there?" The Old Lady could sound so convincingly rational of her terrible behavior towards me. But the pastor's wife insisted that I sit at the table.

What could The Old Lady do?

She was forced to let me sit and eat along with everyone else. For me, this was a miracle! I loved Christmas! I could hear the music and joyful voices singing as we ate. Song after song played as more people arrived and took their seats. We had a good number of people bringing all kinds of wonderful dishes of food. The Old Lady didn't let us stay long and although she tried to keep me so busy serving her, I ate as much as I could.

This is where I learned about the birth of Jesus. Christmas was His birthday and the celebration was all about Him. He was born poor, very poor. As I heard the story, I felt like I could relate to Jesus. My family was very poor. He was also treated unfairly and beaten and punished for things He never did. Jesus really knew what I must be going through because He went through it, too! I loved every minute of the service, although the pastor never did say why we decorate a tree on Jesus' birthday.

Knowing God

I can't say that there was *a moment* that God spoke to me for the first time. I really feel that He has always been with me. When I would cry myself to sleep at night wondering why my mother never came back for me like she promised, He would remind me of what my mother had told me, "Today was a bad day, but tomorrow will be better; rest your head and sleep." I knew somehow God was there; that He would someday give me a better day if I could just hang on. I never hated God in all my troubles, but there were moments I was so very angry with Him. I would vent at God, "Why do you not see? That Old Lady sits in her chair, her Bible open, her lips forming words from what You have written in there and then she screams and yells such terrible things about me! She believes in you? I don't understand."

I always had a voice behind me, "You know it is not right she treats you this way; it was not right for your parents to have sold you," But I never found peace listening to that voice. When I let that attitude stay I was miserable. I was led by these questions: Do I feel good? Do I feel peace?

Deep inside I knew it wasn't God who did this to me; I knew the Bible said to do good things, like love, for I had heard what was written on those pages myself as I sat in church with her, week after week. She might read those words and tell herself she knows the God who wrote them, but His words were words of love and kindness and forgiveness, things she never showed towards me, even though I called her 'Grandma.'

The Gift

Much later I would find out that presents are exchanged on Christmas and I would receive a gift of my own!

It was years later when I first came with The Old Lady to the United States that I would experience what most people think of when they hear the word Christmas: *presents*.

This was my first time in the U.S. We were staying with The Old Lady's Daughter. I had learned to take the verbal and sometimes physical abuse of The Old Lady, but there was another cruelty altogether with her Daughter. If I could explain it, I would almost say there was a jealousy of sorts between us. She was always eyeing me with suspicion, not wanting me to have anything and thinking that I was always trying to manipulate those around me in order to get things, at least that's how it looked to me. Just because it was Christmas, it didn't change how I was treated in the household. I remember it was 2003 and the whole family was there for the holiday. This time, presents were wrapped and placed under the tree. We had never done this in Taiwan. The Old Lady let me set up the tree and decorate it, but she never wrapped presents or gave any to anyone. I saw the boxes tied with bright colored bows in pretty printed paper—such a beautiful sight! It never crossed my mind that one of those boxes would be for me. But when Christmas Day came, The Old Lady, her Daughter and their family opened the gifts. I was always with the family or at least a family member, not because I was a member or a part of them at all, it was more on the lines of being watched. So of course I was there, watching the presents being opened while I cooked or prepared something for The Old Lady. I was moving on my feet all day long, never allowed to sit or rest at all. I was watching them unwrap presents while I fixed The Old Lady her daily fresh juice when I heard The Old Lady's grandson call my name from the room that the family was all gathered in. I could see Allison; The Old Lady's grandson's girlfriend was motioning for me to come near. I did not know her very well, and although everyone knew that I was not a true member of the family, I think some felt sorry that I was treated so poorly. I turned the juicer off and walked silently towards her. "What do they need now?" I said to myself.

Allison was crouched near the tree reaching towards a box that had been pushed towards the back, deep under the tree. Bending on one knee she carefully picked it up and held it out towards me. I reached for it, still having no idea that she was actually giving it to ME. As I pulled the box closer, I saw the tag had my name on it and said, "From: Allison." I blankly stared at it, wondering what I was supposed to do next. "It's for you," Allison gently whispered. I was stunned. My heart began to race. "Would I get in trouble for this?" I thought, all the while excited to get my first Christmas present! I felt the stares of The Old Lady and her Daughter as I carefully tore open the pretty red and white paper and untied the green ribbon. Absentmindedly, I let the paper fall to the ground forgetting I would be the one to clean up the mess of wrapping paper and boxes. I pulled at the tape that held the box lid shut and peeled it off with my finger. I lifted the lid slowly and saw the glint of something gold. Remembering the wrapping that fell, I tucked the lid under the box and pulled back the tissue paper. It was small and golden with a faint sparkly shine to it. A purse! A purse of my very own! I felt like a princess.

For a brief moment I felt an explosion of joy, but it was just a moment. The Old Lady's Daughter could not bear to see me happy for a second. "What do YOU need with a purse?!" she exclaimed. "What could you possibly have to put into a purse? No, no…you don't need such a thing…" Suddenly, I felt the blood rush to my face…I was so embarrassed! My first real gift and I felt ashamed to have it. Why did they have to ruin this moment? I grasped the purse and dropped the box to the floor with the rest of wrapping and ran to the bathroom.

I locked the door and began crying uncontrollably. I can't explain it, but I just came undone. I bawled so hard my face was red and puffy and wet with tears. At that moment I felt so worthless, so empty—every part of me hurt. What was so horrible about treating me like a human being? I tried so hard every single day to serve this family, to please them, to do what they wanted me to do and I am not allowed to enjoy one moment? Was it wrong to have something of my own? I held the purse to my chest. I felt the heat in my face again but this time it was in anger. Wiping my face with a towel, I made a decision: I was going to carry that purse! It didn't matter if I had one thing to put in it, I was going to keep it and carry it.

In the days that followed The Daughter continued, relentlessly to shame me, "What do you want from Allison that she gave you that purse? I know you, using her to get what you want!" Day after day, whenever she saw me with that purse, the taunting would start until I broke and could no longer carry the purse in front of her. One day it just disappeared. I never knew what happened to it.

Revenge

I guess there were things I could do to get my revenge on The Old Lady and those in her family that treated me so badly. But being so stubborn, I wasn't going to let them turn me to evil! I did not meditate on such thoughts because they made me sick…and besides, by the time I lay my head down on the floor at night to sleep, I was too exhausted to think about anything!

There was just something still so hopeful about Christmas that had always stayed with me no matter where I found myself. Whether the holiday comes and goes without a tree or presents, just the hint of it in the air around makes me smile.

Chapter 9

The Call

"You can't have more money, if that's what your father is thinking...I won't do it! I paid over $10,000 NTD, and for what?! A scrawny, useless girl who is more trouble at times than she is worth?! If that's not why you called, then what do you want?!" I had heard the heated words as I was in the bedroom making The Old Lady's bed and tidying her room. I was curious as to who she was talking to, but I learned to mind my own business and never ask questions. I tugged at my shirt that was now so short on me that my skin showed just above my hips. My pants were becoming so tight that just bending to smooth out the blankets, caused them to pull on me, shorting my reach. My clothes were always way too big or much too small—but I was grateful, at least there were no holes in them—at least not yet.

"What do you want me to do about it? I cannot spare to let her go for any length of time...who will do all the work that needs to be done?!" The conversation continued, but The

Old Lady was clearly upset about something and I was pretty sure that something had to do with me. Suddenly the shouting stopped and I heard The Old Lady footsteps stomping towards the bedroom.

My Father Is Dead

"Your father is dead." The Old Lady blurted out, unemotionally. "Your family has called to request you be sent to attend the funeral, but you will not stay the required time. I will not have you gone more than for the day of the funeral," she went on in an angry tone. "I cannot go with you, so I will send someone with you." She turned and walked out of the room. I stood there, hit by this news. This was July of 1994, I was about fourteen years old. I hadn't seen my dad since he had driven me to Taipei to live with The Old Lady, promising me he would return, and never did. I was so angry—at him, at my mom—to be left with this horrible lady. But he *was* my father. He was dead. I never had the chance to tell him my anger, to reason with him to be brought back home, to cry and beg him to bring me to my mother. I started to remember that last day with my family. Tears began to fill my eyes, but I could not let The Old Lady see them.

The Phone Calls

I had no idea that The Old Lady had kept in touch with my family. Yes, there were a few times that I knew my father had called because The Old Lady would put me on the phone, and like some kidnapped victim, I was only allowed to say, "Hello, father," then the phone was taken away from me. She would tell me later that my dad was calling only to ask for more money, but I didn't believe her. Once when she handed me the phone I was able to quickly say, "Hello, Father...Please, I want to come home," but then she snatched the receiver out of my hand and shouted at me to leave the room.

I guess all those years she had also written to my family from time to time, including pictures of me, letting them know that I was okay and that I 'loved' my life with her. She told them lies that I would never return and that I didn't want to ever see them again. I had no idea that they had also contacted her, hoping to see me or reconnect in some way, but she never showed me any letters, never told me of any *those* calls, and of course she never told me they had known, all along, where I was. I believed her when she'd said they didn't want me and had never tried to come see me. Why shouldn't I believe her? Selling me to her was a fact. And besides, they promised to come and bring me home. They had broken that promise.

The Funeral

I could not be sent to my father's funeral alone. The Old Lady would not allow that! Her son's girlfriend would go with me, making sure to keep me in tow, and bring me home as soon as possible. I didn't have the proper clothes for a funeral, and of course none would be given to me, so I went with what I had. The girlfriend called for a taxi to take us to the train station and we made the long journey back towards my home village. The Old Lady's lies about my family filled me with doubts about them. "They sold you. If you go back, they will just sell you again," she had said one day. This was true. They *did* sell me. Although those first days and months I had missed them so much, time had brought anger and hate to me and I often battled them both at night as I lay on the cold hard floor, with my head on my pillow of smelly rags, thinking about home. Sometimes I imagined myself shouting at my parents, pronouncing judgement on the terrible thing they did by selling me. I wished, at times, for awful things to happen to them, only regretting it all as I finally fell asleep. I never had love for my father. Now he was dead. My heart was torn inside. He was my father, after all.

My dad, who was an alcoholic, had been killed in an accident. One morning he had been drinking heavily, got on his motorcycle to drive home and lost control. His motorcycle spun around out of control and smashed into a wall. It was a very bad accident. I remembered my dad's temper, his rash ways of dealing with circumstances in life. I remember how he treated my mother. I thought of my mother and sisters. Tears fell down my face as I looked out the window of train and we came closer to our stop.

I was not allowed to get too close to my family at the funeral. Everyone was crying as I stood there, like a bystander. The moment did not seem real. The details are so hard to recall, so hazy. I knew my family was upset that I would not stay for the required amount of days. Our culture required it, but how could I tell them I was watched by the son's girlfriend and couldn't stay. The Old Lady would find out and it would be bad for me. We stayed just a few hours before I was forced to leave. I can still see my sisters crying, my mother standing there. I was so guarded and untrusting of them. It kept me from reaching out to them; telling them what had happened to me. Sometimes I wish I could go back and do things differently, but I can't. We took a taxi from there and stayed the night not far from the village and then headed back to Taipei early the next morning. I would not see any of my family again for another eighteen years.

Dawu Township.

First pair of shoes Judy bought me.   *My father's grave site.*

135

First time I went to see my family again when I was free.

Section II

Chapter 10

Big Changes

The Old Lady's Daughter had lived in the United States for many years. She had married an American and done pretty well for herself. They had owned several businesses and had property. I remember when I was much younger, The Old Lady went to stay with her daughter for several months in the U.S. while I stayed with The Old Lady's sister. I was always 'kept' by someone, never alone. In 2000, however, I travelled to the U.S. with The Old Lady on what was supposed to be a six-month visit. I, of course, cooked and cleaned and waited on the woman hand and foot; it wasn't a vacation for me. I was always introduced to others as a 'granddaughter' and that is how inquiries were avoided and I was able move so freely and travel with this family. I guess this could have been an adventure to me as well, but it turned into a nightmare!

This was the first time I had ever left Taiwan. The trip quickly took a horribly wrong turn when I suddenly became extremely sick. It must've been the dry air or change in humidity that brought it all on. The weather just seemed to affect me badly. My skin became very dry and cracked. It felt itchy and a rash covered my entire body; my legs were the most effected. This was extremely painful and soon open sores began to form where the dry irritated skin had split open. I suppose it was an act of kindness on The Daughter's part to give me some lotion to put on it. But even the acts of kindness were tainted with selfish cruelties. The lotion was old and expired. I twisted off the lid and my nose caught a faint unpleasant smell. What could I do? My legs were in excruciating pain and this was all I had. I squeezed a small dab of the slightly yellow substance into my palm and carefully rubbed it into my wounds. It stung a little, but I continued dabbing the lotion on my legs until I covered every dry and cracked patch. I felt no relief. The next morning my legs felt hot and tight and when I turned up my pant legs I saw a reddish ring forming on the edges of the sores. I put more of the lotion on my legs. I did this for over two and a half weeks until the lotion was nearly gone. My legs only grew worse. In addition to the redness, I noticed considerable swelling—eventually getting so bad, I could barely get my pants to fit and my skin began to secrete a clear sticky substance.

Something is Wrong

Each day the pain grew more intense. It became progressively harder and harder just to walk and move around and especially hard to sit or stand. My chores and routine did not change. I still had to get up at 5 a.m. to cook and clean and take care of the family. I did this slower than usual and without sympathy, just disapproving glares. One morning as I led The Old Lady on her early morning walk to the park, a neighbor called to us as we walked past her, "Your granddaughter... her legs...why are her pants so wet and her legs so swollen?! Show me your legs young lady." The woman was watching us as she watered her lawn. She often made conversation with us as our paths intersected. "It's best to water before the sun gets too hot. A good time to walk as well," she'd say. It was not idle chit chat today. The Old Lady could not avoid her, she had to stop. I was wearing these purple pants and walking rather stiff legged because of the pain. The sores were oozing the clear fluid, wet and sticky, visible through my pants, which were now wet and clinging to my legs unnaturally. I cautiously peeled my pant legs up to show the woman my swollen and infected legs. She gasped at the sight and blurted out, "You need to take her to the doctor right away!" I could sense the anger rising in The Old Lady. Her embarrassment that someone had noticed me and a need that I had made her furious. The words stumbled out of her mouth, tumbling clumsily to concoct some reasonable explanation as to why I was in the condition I was in. She made no real sense and mumbled a final, "Yes, she will see my doctor very soon," to the woman and we hurriedly turned around and headed back to the house.

We were barely inside when The Old Lady unleashed a wave of insults, "What is wrong with you?! Why have you let this happen?! Now I will have to take you to see my doctor... how will you pay for this? You don't have any money. You will not be able to pay me, you lazy girl!" she ranted, "See, I told you that you were trouble, always causing trouble. You are lucky that I ever took you in! No one wants you, no one will ever want you!" The words she spoke dug deep into my heart, wounding me much deeper than the oozing, weeping sores on my legs. I ran off to the bathroom and closed the door and cried.

The Doctor

A few days later we were able to get in to see the doctor. Both The Old Lady and I went into the examination room and waited. After some time the doctor came in. The Old Lady spoke for me as I was told to roll up my pant legs. I wore the same purple pants, I had no others at the time. When he saw my condition he was appalled and afraid to touch my legs. "Oh my gosh!" he said, thinking my horrific rash may be contagious. He studied my legs, his eyes digging intently into every inch, trying hard not to get too close and touch them.

After a few moments he asked, "Were you using anything...soap...that could have caused this? Stop using whatever you may be putting on them immediately." I told him how itchy my legs were and about the lotion that I was given and what had happened. He listened all the while never taking his eyes off of my legs, nodding his head in acknowledgement without turning away from this gruesome sight. He opened a drawer and rattled its contents around until he found what he was looking for and filled a syringe, placing a large needle on the top. "This should help somewhat..." His voice trailed off. He gave me the shot and a prescription for more antibiotics. I didn't have insurance or money to pay him, so The Old Lady was forced to pay. Although she complained under her breathe, she paid him. Firmly she asked, "What about travel? We have just a few more weeks and then we must return to Taiwan." A look of concern fell over his face. He was worried about my welfare. "She needs rest. I will need to see her again to make sure she is healing up properly. She cannot travel until then," he turned away and scribble the prescription on a pad of paper. I felt relieved. I knew that my daily workload would not change, and rest was unlikely but finally healing was beginning in my body. I took in a deep breath and let it out slowly. I cautiously pulled my pant legs down and slid off the cold metal table.

Though the air was charged with anger and frustration, silence followed us on the ride home. Wheels were turning in The Old Lady's mind. She would arrange for her Daughter to finagle my travel visa to be extended another six months. It was a long six months. I eventually healed but I still have scars on my legs.

When we returned to Taiwan, life continued as usual.

Chapter 11

America

I had begun to notice subtle changes in The Old Lady. She had always been mean towards me, but her actions became more and more bizarre. I was used to doing a chore and having her displeased. This was my life. I was never good enough for her. I remember once a visit from a woman who had apparently been a servant of hers before I had come along. The Old Lady was so sweet to her, recounting memories of her service with fondness, all the while I stood there, waiting for a command, hearing her compare me to this woman. "And *this* one!" she shot a glance my way. "So useless! Much too little and incompetent!" They continued to visit, drinking tea and laughing from time to time. When the visitor had left, I began to clear away the dishes to wash them. The Old Lady walked over to me.

"Did you enjoy eavesdropping on us, thief?" She reached out her hand and grabbed my breast, right at the nipple, and pinched it as hard as she could with her fingers. I winched in pain and dropped a small plate that contained scraps of pastry left over from tea. The plate fell to the floor and broke into pieces. "You lazy careless child!" she screamed and slapped me across the face. "You won't eat those scraps now as your lunch, Throw them in the trash…and I will check to make sure they stay there!" I rubbed my breast as I knelt on the ground, picking up the pieces of the broken plate and pastry crumbs that were scattered on the floor. The Old Lady had never pinched me like this before, and it began to happen more and more often. Her suspicions of me grew and her behavior became extremely erratic. I wasn't sure how old she was, but I knew she must be in her late 80's. Things seemed to get worse as she got older. She began to kick me and accuse me of ridiculous things. She was becoming crazy and had more violent outbursts.

"Please, Grandma…Don't!"

"This pot had *plenty* of tea left in it. That thieving girl!" The Old Lady shouted from the kitchen. My heart jumped at those words. I was clearing away the rest of the dishes from the table after all of her guests had left. They enjoyed a wonderful lunch of chicken, sticky rice balls and tea and I stood serving or waiting to serve just like I always did. I knew I would probably be slapped, but I fearfully walked into the kitchen to face The Old Lady's anger.

"Grandma, what is wrong? I did not drink any of your tea. You saw me the whole time your friends were here…when could I have done this? I did not, I wouldn't steal your tea!" My voice cracked as I knew there would be some punishment, but I didn't expect what happened next.

"I will not stand for this from a slave like you!" she screamed. Her eyes seethed with such rage, I was taken by surprise for a brief moment. Suddenly, she grabbed me by the hair and pulled me so hard I fell to the ground. I was caught off guard and scrambled to get up, but I couldn't. She held on tight and continued to yank and twist my hair so violently that I flopped back and forth on the floor. Her strength in doing this was beyond what I was used to and I didn't know what to do but cry, "Please, Grandma! I swear I didn't drink your tea! How could I? Please, please, don't hurt me like this…ahhh… please! My neck! Ouch…Grandma!"

I begged and begged her to stop but she was like a machine. Her grip tightened and she began to drag me down the hall. I reached up, trying to pull her fingers off of my hair, but it was impossible. I slid on the tile but when she reached the carpet, she grabbed me with both hands and pulled even harder, dragging me forcefully further down the hall. My dress bunched up around my waist and my bare bottom scraped against the course fibers and burned as it tore my skin. I screamed out in pain as The Old Lady yanked me into the bathroom. I collapsed in a heap, my arm hitting the base of the toilet. Oh, how I hurt all over! Thinking this horrible scene was done, I sat up. That is when The Old Lady jerked the brush used to clean the toilet from its stand and began to shove it into my mouth! I grit my teeth to keep it out but my lips and gums

147

surrounding my face were rubbed raw from the harsh bristles of the brush. "That will teach you to take what is not yours!" She hissed. She now had one hand on my shirt trying to force my face towards the filthy toilet brush. She shoved it again and again at my mouth until she was satisfied and then pushed me down and threw the brush at my head. "And clean this mess up or I'll make things will be worse for you!" she commanded and she stomped back down the hall towards the kitchen.

A small drop of blood dripped down my chin; one of the bristles had punctured the inside of my lower lip. I sobbed as I sat there. I was in such pain it took a long time for me to stand up. When I did, I looked in the mirror and I rinsed my mouth out carefully. My cheeks were puffy and my eyes red from crying so hard. My throat felt sore. It must've been the screams, begging her to stop. I peeled my skirt up to see the raw spot were the rug had burned me. I dabbed it with a piece wet tissue. My head was so sore and my neck ached. I couldn't turn it without stabbing pain on either side. But it was inside where I hurt the most. This woman, this 'grandma' of mine hated me so. Why did she hate me? Why couldn't I please her? I wanted to be loved so very badly by her. She was the only family I had. I knew I had to clean up the mess in the bathroom, but I cried and cried the whole time.

Moving to the U.S.

I was about seventeen years old when The Old Lady told me, "We are going to live in the United States. My daughter wants me to come. I will not have a slave there, so you will come live with us, to take care of me. Things will not change for you; you are a slave and will always be a slave," she said, pounding her authoritative words into me. The Old Lady's daughter was concerned now that her mother was getting older and wanted me to continue to take care of her but live in the U.S. with her and her husband. My previous trip there was not a good experience, so I was afraid. I didn't have any travel papers or anything, so somehow this family was going to get me there. I don't remember how much longer we stayed in Taiwan after this, maybe a year or so, but I remember wondering if my family knew where I was now, and that I was going to be living in the U.S.

The Daughter had come to Taiwan several times in order to arrange all the travel plans, taking me to sign papers, having pictures of me taken, many things which I cannot now recall. The Old Lady and her Daughter always made sure things looked perfect. I was always happy and willing to anyone who would question otherwise. Did I have a choice? Was this the life I had chosen? I just did what they wanted. What could I do? I was never to say no, ever. When things were all in place, it was time to start boxing things up. The building belonged to The Old Lady's son, so most of The Old Lady's possessions could be boxed up and stored there, but she would want to go through what she thought was necessary to bring with her to her new home in the states.

Packing

I helped The Old Lady pack while movers took care of any other possessions she planned on taking. The Old Lady trusted my skills in picking out her outfits—the one thing she didn't criticize me for—so I chose a few of her favorites and placed them carefully in her suitcase. I thought about what I owned that would go with me. I had no clothes to speak of and was never allowed to buy anything for myself, but I did have a Bible. A church member had given it to me as a gift. "This book contains the very words of God. He spoke them to us all, and it still speaks to us, if we just listen," the kind Christian explained. I looked at the black leather worn cover. Two gold colored words were written across the front. Although I couldn't read it, I promised myself, one day, I would read this book. "Thank you so much," I said as I bowed slightly, holding my new treasure. This was my only possession. I would keep this with me.

Becoming 'Sharon'

When everything was packed up and the movers had taken what things The Old Lady had wanted, The Daughter turned to me with a stern look and said, "You say nothing at the airport—at customs, you hear me? You will nod and only agree with what I or my mother say, understand?" She grabbed my shoulders tightly as she said, "Understand?" I knew this was important and I was not to disobey her or things would be very bad for me. The Daughter's words were always so cutting and poisonous to me, but she never touched or hurt me like The Old Lady did. "You are now to be called, 'Sharon'—this is now your name—SHARON. We will be living as Americans now." I felt her firm grip and knew I was to go along *with everything*. I had been with this family since I was seven years old. Yes, I was a slave, sold to them, but I was also a part of their family, a terrible, abusive family, but I was a part of it. Where could I go if I left? What would happened if I spoke up? The fear and inability to know what I would do kept me in this place.

So I came to live in the U.S. It was such a big place! Where Taipei was busy with motorcycles, buses, and people crammed everywhere, the U.S. was more spread out. There were still buses, people and cars—so many cars—but the streets were huge! The neighborhoods so much different than where I had lived. The house I lived in here with The Old Lady and her daughter was nice. Carpet was on all the floors and they had a backyard with grass and trees and flowers. The weather was much drier, and I had remembered what had happened on my first trip.

Maybe things will be better here, I thought.

The Workload Gets Heavier

When I lived with The Old Lady in Taiwan, I did all of the work. I cleaned her very large apartment building where she forced me to mop, scrub, cook, clean, wash dishes, mend clothes, and do laundry. I took care of her personally as well, making her tea, bathing her, dressing her, cooking for her and her son. I woke up at 5 a.m. and helped her do her exercises and we routinely made the journey to Yang Ming Shan. I would be exhausted, going to bed late at night after massaging The Old Lady's feet and hands. Here in the U.S. I was still expected to take care of The Old Lady, the house, AND The Old Lady's Daughter and her husband! I still awoke every morning at 5 a.m., but I was expected to adjust all of my chores to the schedule of the rest of the household. Things got worse when it was decided that I would go to work with The Daughter and help run her store. "My mother will go with us to the store and you will come to look after her," The Daughter had said. But most of the time, The Old Lady was put in a back room to watch TV while I cleaned the store. I would sweep, vacuum, clean the bathroom, take out the trash, set up and put away items in the shop and do whatever errands I was told to do by The Daughter. As soon as we got home in the evening, which would be 6 p.m. or later, I hurried to cook them all dinner and then tend to The Old Lady's needs again, going to sleep almost regularly at 1 a.m. The Old Lady had a large bed, but I was forced to sleep on the floor in her room, in case she needed help in the middle of the night.

Most seventeen-year-old girls are giggly and so happy in life. They have boyfriends, hang out with friends, maybe stay long after school to do cheerleading or participate in some sport or club. Not me. I felt old and tired. I got only little glimpses of what girls my age did, but I knew how they looked and dressed when The Daughter's son's girlfriend, Kim, would come over. I noticed everything about her—how she dressed and what make-up she wore.

I was careful not to let The Daughter catch me looking too long at anything. She watched me like a hawk and used any excuse to humiliate me and tear me down. "You like Kim's cute skirt, huh?" She said slyly one day after she saw me look-ing at her. "You can't wear that skirt, you know. Your butt is so big! I am ashamed even to have you out front of my shop—you ugly thing! You are chasing customers away with the way you look." She continued her sharp cutting comments with a look of such distaste on her face. "…You can't even speak En-glish…What is wrong with you, you stupid girl? No one will ever find a use for you…"

Every day was filled with work to do. I never got a day off or even a moment to rest. Sundays were especially hard because by then I was so tired from the week and the family expected me to serve them on their day off! They didn't want to do anything for themselves, especially on Sunday.

My Only Friend

"Pick up these dog messes in the backyard now!" demand-ed The Daughter early one Sunday morning. "My mother will want to get to church on time so you had better get it done, you lazy girl!" I had just finished cooking breakfast for The Daughter and her husband and had started on cleaning up the dishes. "Uhhhh…" I whispered as I set the towel down and hurried to the sliding glass door.

The family had a little backyard with flowers in it. The Daughter's son had this really big dog and she let him keep him there in the backyard. After breakfast, usually, I would feed the dog and water the flowers outside. I did this every morning. I would pick up dog messes, water the plants and any gardening that was needed. Out here was the only place I could be alone with my thoughts. I would try to look busy outside so I could think. "How long until this is all over?" I'd wonder. "I want to be free." I would wish for someone to take care of me. I had lots of wishes: I wanted to go to school, to go out and have fun like normal people. I would imagine this family would change and treat me better, like a real family. Every day I wish my life was better, and that I could feel pretty. Out of all of the chore I did—the only one that I liked was playing with the dog and feeding him. All other chores I did like a robot. I had to do them. But I loved that dog. He liked me, too. He was my best friend for he listened to me talk about all my troubles.

As I started to unlock the door, I glanced down at all the shoes lined up in pairs just on the other side of it. I noticed one of The Daughter's shoes was missing. "Here boy, come, come on boy..." I called, looking for the big beautiful Husky. Although I loved this huge gentle giant of a dog, so often I had to cover up for his behavior. He liked to steal a shoe or two when he could and chew them up. He'd taken one of The Old Lady's shoes once and of course, I was yelled at as much as the dog was for taking it. Today I was sure he'd gotten hold of The Daughter's sandal. "Here boy..." I called again. I walked towards the shovel, searching for his 'messes' as I often did. He was such a good dog. As much as he loved chewing shoes he never stole mine. Once The Old Lady commented, "Why does he never chew your sandals?" Everyone in that house had had a shoe torn up by him—but not me! I was so thankful because

I only had one pair of shoes. How he knew this, I didn't know. If he'd chewed mine, I'd have to wear them just as they were.

He's Gone!

I picked up the shovel and carefully scooped up a rather large doggie mess and headed to the bucket which I had lined with a trash bag. Disposing of it, I put the lid on the bucket and turned around. "NO!" I shouted. The gate on the side of the yard was open and the dog was missing! I hurriedly looked all over the yard calling his name, but he was gone. I ran towards the house to grab some dog treats and leash, hoping to coax the dog to come to me, if I found him. He would often escape, running out the side gate if it wasn't latched tight and I would get blamed because I would take the trash cans out that gate once a week. I couldn't go after him because I wasn't allowed to walk the dog alone, or even be out front without permission. I dashed out the side yard anyway and ran towards the front of the house. Where could he be? Down towards the end of the street, sniffing a large bush with great interest, was the dog! Relieved yet still a bit nervous he might run, I called to him sweetly, "Come baby, come to me," I continue to repeat this in the direction of the huge beast as I walked slowly and calmly towards him. "I have a doggie treat for you." I said. "A crunchy treat. Mmm. Taste good." I coaxed. He turned his head and walked over to me. He sniffed the treat and began munching the biscuit and covering my hand in drool. I carefully clicked his leash onto his collar. Suddenly, he pulled away and nearly dragged me down on the sidewalk!

I had to pull him as hard as I could, for he did NOT want to come back home with me. He was so heavy and strong, but somehow I was able to get him back in the yard before anyone knew he was missing.

The Daughter

I continued to cook for the family. They would eat first and I would eat last. Whatever was leftover, I was given that. The dog was given more food than I got. I was treated worse than a dog! I never drank much milk. I made it by mixing it from a powder in those days. The Daughter's son liked milk with his oatmeal. Every morning I made oatmeal for him. If I accidently spilled any of it while cooking I would scoop it up and taste it. The Daughter would always say to me, "Do not steal my son's food," Whether I did or not I would still get scolded or punished. I would cry at some point every day for what was said or done to me. The Daughter would cook eggs for her son once in a while and give me the yolks and say, "Here, eat it," and I would eat it because I was so hungry. Even if food had been in the fridge and it turned sour I still would eat it. I can't stand to eat the yolks today, only scrambled eggs.

New Clothes

I do remember once asking for some new clothes or some money to get some. I was never given anything special. I continued to wear the same clothes day after day. People from church who saw me donated clothes to me. I once wore the same pair of shoes for three years, they were these open toed type sandals. I never even knew my own shoe size, so I was excited when The Daughter said yes.

I was taken to a discount store and I could choose something under five dollars. I was actually able to find a few things but when I began to wear them I was made fun of. "Oh, you think you look so pretty in your new clothes, do you?" The Daughter said one day in that jealous sounding voice she had. "Wanting men to pay attention to you, eh? Are you going to flirt to get a boyfriend with your new clothes?" I felt guilty for having something nice. I felt overwhelmed with shame. I didn't know what they said was wrong. I thought they must be right or why would they say those things?

Alone in America

I was never allowed to forge any close relationships with anyone for fear I might discover the truth—or that others would, so I was *never* left alone. They were always with me. I never socialized with anyone but them. I had thought about escaping, but how could I? I didn't know where to go. If they catch me, I thought, it will be worse! After many months of being in America, The Daughter needed more and more help at her work. I didn't speak any English and this was beginning to be a problem.

"I want you to spend time on this computer to learn English," she told me one day.

"There is this program where you can learn—you just put a CD in here," she motioned to the box (hard drive, as I was told), "and it will come up on the screen. Do this when you are finished with your chores." Finished with my chores? I thought. When am I ever finished with my chores! Most of the time I'd be half asleep and doing a chore, or doing one for The Old Lady and The Daughter would interrupt me to do one for her. I was forever doing chores and now I would have to find time to do this! Once or twice, well after midnight, I'd try to study English this way, but it was not very often.

Being in America and living in a large house I hoped I would have a bed to sleep in. The Old Lady had an extra room with a bed in it back in Taiwan, but I was still forced to sleep on the floor. Maybe here things would be different.

At first The Old Lady did ask me, "Come sleep in the bed." Maybe it was because she was so old and got cold at night, I don't know, but I welcomed those times. When The Daughter saw this she would not allow it. Once, The Daughter had come into her mother's bedroom for some reason, and saw her mother was not in bed but I was. She questioned me, "Little sister," she scolded in Chinese, "Why do you not help her? She is in the bathroom alone without help. Now you must always sleep on the floor!" From then on if the Old Lady got up to use the bathroom, I would have to get up too because she would step on me when getting out of bed.

The Forever Lie

The family continued to hide my identity. If anyone asked who I was in church, or anywhere, it was, "This is my granddaughter or Goddaughter." I feel like my life was a lie…they fabricated everything. No one wanted to get involved, so they would never question why I was with them or who I really was. They kept everyone distant from me. I would get slapped later if I took food offered to me from church members. "Why you waste this food? You are fed at home!" I was told, if we were at a potluck or event.

The Daughter's husband once saw that I was sad. He was American and asked me, "Why are you crying, Sharon?" He knew of course what was going on but never said anything. He knew I was a slave. He saw how I was treated. I didn't answer him, but later The Daughter found out he had spoken to me. She came storming down from upstairs and confronted me, "You are so evil; you threaten our marriage, you whore! I know you are trying to seduce my husband!" she accused me. She would say horrible things to me in Chinese and then end by saying, "It doesn't matter what you wear or how you dress—you are a slave; you will always be a slave." I hated her when she said this but I just sat there crying. I had no fight in me. I was empty inside.

Dreaded Shopping

I hated to go shopping with The Daughter. I couldn't read English at all so finding the exact items she wanted always ended up with her shouting at me, "Are you stupid! You can't figure anything out on your own?" The Daughter became more verbally abusive as time went on. I think this started with The Old Lady. I overheard her talking with her daughter saying, "Sharon, I believe, is flirting with your husband." Why The Old Lady said these things I don't know. Was it on purpose to create problems for me or was she getting so senile and paranoid that she truly believed this about me? I don't know, but The Daughter's horrid comments to me cut me deeply.

There were times at the shop it was so busy that I was allowed to pick up lunch for The Old Lady and her Daughter. They would call the order in and I walked (just a few doors down from where we worked) to the restaurant to pick it up. I was never allowed to order a lunch for myself but ate what The Old Lady did not finish. I hated how she always placed her chewed leftovers on top of any untouched food on the bottom. She did this on purpose so I would have to pick up the discards—bones, skin, half bitten pieces, spat out fatty chunks—in order to eat any rice or noodles that had not been touched underneath. I HATED THIS.

I was doing more and more work at the shop—working with customers or standing out front, to bring customers in. I know people witnessed the cruelness of this family for The Old Lady had trouble hiding it at work. Once, when she was mad about something, she grabbed her cane and hit me on the back of the legs. She hit me so hard I nearly fell over. Several people turned to see what had happened. But nobody said a word. It seemed to only give a boldness to the cruel behavior of these women. The Daughter now berated me more publicly without shame and was overheard by other shop owners to have said, "You, dumb, stupid girl! No wonder you're only a servant." As they saw me crying many times. Too scared to come forward, they stayed silent and I stay a slave.

Chapter 12

Judy

It had now become a regular task for me to go with the Old Lady and her Daughter to help out at her business—clean the restrooms, sweep, and vacuum, do whatever she needed before the shop opened. Like most of the work I was forced to do, it began in the early morning hours long before the sun had fully awakened. I lived in a constant state of exhaustion—working eighteen to twenty hours a day! I had become numb to the routine chores, I did them mechanically, my body going through the motions, my heart and head someplace else. I got up and dressed in the same tattered outfit I always wore and after serving my captors needs, listlessly got into the car as I was told.

We arrived at the shop just before 6 a.m. The Daughter hurriedly pushed me towards the open shop door. "You, go… clean the workshop and toilets before the men arrive. Sweep and get rid of the trash. Hurry. Customers will come." I gathered my cleaning supplies together and trudged toward the workshop. The workshop was a long narrow room that contained a telephone, restrooms, and a small workbench and chair. If something needed repair it could be done there. It was cramped and dusty and dark; no windows to see in or out of, and the door could be locked from the inside. I began my daily chores here. Cleaning the room and disposing of the trash. The restrooms were always filthy. They were the only ones in the building and everyone used them. I finished the sweeping and carted my supplies into the men's room and began scrubbing the toilets. So often I felt like I was dead and yet alive at the same time. Did I hate scouring these disgusting toilets more than mopping the floors? I felt nothing. I could feel my heart beating, but I cleaned like I was dead; uncaring what the chore was or how long it would take. Why should I care? That would not change anything. Every day was filled with burdens that would be repeated again tomorrow. Maybe today would have a little less trouble. I could at least feel some measure of hope in that.

When I finished with the workroom and toilets, I started on the rest of the building: vacuuming, dusting, cleaning. I had been doing this task now for quite some time, day after day, month after month and no one who came in ever asked, "Who are you and why do you do this?" When the tenants who rented out the sections of the shop set up their wares they looked at me quizzically, but never said a word. I saw in their eyes the recognition that something wasn't right. They saw how I was treated. They heard The Old Lady's cutting words to me all the while calling me, 'Granddaughter,' but they stayed silent. Only their eyes spoke to me. "I know something is wrong here, but it is not my place to say; I cannot get involved in this." So my life dragged on, slowly forward like a beast of burden under the power of the whip.

Gradually I was allowed to do other jobs, such as helping to set up merchandise in the displays. I was around more people when I did this but always under the suspicious eye of The Old Lady or her Daughter. I was happy that I could be out front; hearing and seeing other people. It kept my mind off sad thoughts and held back the cruelest words from my captors. It was in doing this new task that I met Judy. Though most of the renters were of Asian or Middle Eastern decent, Judy was not. She stood out in the way she dressed and in how she spoke—with a kindness that was both compassionate and strong. Her short brown hair was styled purposefully at her shoulders and her eyes saw me in a way the others did not.

Unexpected Friendship

I noticed Judy from the first moment she walked in the door. There was something about this woman that was electric. Her style was elegant yet understated enough to make her approachable. Her hair was beautiful, her make-up flawless. Her face had always the hint of a smile. Not a person could walk by unnoticed nor unsolicited by her. "Hello, how are you today?" she'd call out even if she were already in the middle of a conversation at the moment. "Treating the Misses right, I hope," she'd say to a potential customer in a friendly way. "I have the perfect gift that says, 'I love you,'" she'd coax. It was hard not to notice Judy—or feel like she was your best friend. I felt that way as well and even though the watchful eyes of The Old Lady and her Daughter were upon me, I would sneak in a smile or wave to her when I could. And she, being the friendly woman she was, would do the same. There were times I was drawn to talk to her, but I would change my route at the last minute out of fear of punishment from my captors. Something had begun to change in me—the day Judy came in to my life was like a light and rays of hope slowly began to pierce the darkness I felt each day.

Judy's Past

Judy had lived several lives of her own by this time. She had grown up in a wealthy community, but as impressive as that was it was not an ideal life. Her mother had divorced and remarried, and her stepfather had his favorites out of his three children, and she being his only stepchild, was not one of them. He had owned several restaurants in the posh area surrounding this wealthy community, yet Judy never ate there for free. Maybe it was then that the idea to make enough money so she would never feel second-hand again, began. She did manage to marry well on her second time around and was now working side by side with Darrin, so they could afford the finer things in life, which consisted of a mansion-sized home not far from a well-known wealthy hot spot, near the beach. But there are things that money can't buy.

Judy's husband, Darrin, had been sick for long time. His heart and lungs had slowed the energetic and active man he was at one time. Judy ran the business more and more these days, as he became too sick to do it. It was in this time of transitioning from a full-time business to a more temporary one that brought Judy in to my life. Downsizing from their own once profitable trade, she had rented out a small area in the building The Old Lady's Daughter owned and set up shop. Darrin was too ill on many days to even get out of the car, so it was Judy who carried in her wares, encouraging customers to buy, and packed things up at the end of the day. She did this five to seven days a week.

The whole downstairs of the shop was filled with vendors who paid rent to use a small section and sell their goods. Judy had rented such a space and was selling her own products to those who wandered through this 'flea market' of sorts. Her tables were set up with beautiful things. I often stole a glance as I walked past her section. She had noticed me, too, but unlike the others, she had decided one day to cross the gulf between us. "Hi. What is your name?" She asked me one day. I could not speak very much English at the time and understanding it was extremely difficult. I knew I would be in trouble if I was seen talking to anyone in a personal way, so I gave a brief nod and said, 'Sharon.' I kept my head down, attentively working. I had no idea at the time the significance of that first conversation. I don't think anyone did.

The Gifts

Business did not go as well as Judy hoped, but that didn't stop her from being generous. The woman loved to shop but she loved getting deals all the more. It wasn't unusual for her to buy her expensive Lancôme make-up products without walking away with a second set for free. One of these times, she handed that free selection to The Old Lady's Daughter. "I have noticed your…is she your granddaughter…that helps you each day. She has beautiful skin, but I wonder if she might like some make-up to bring out those gorgeous eyes of hers. I don't want to seem forward, but will you give this to her as a gift, from me?" That hint of a smile grew wide as Judy handed the expensive gift to her. The Daughter of course took it and thanked her for the kindness, for who wouldn't? It would be months later that I would learn that this wasn't the only gift Judy had given to me via The Daughter that never made it into my hands, more would be given with that same generous smile, yet not one gift would I see. Still, Judy had no clue what was happening behind the scenes.

I could say a few words in English, but any communication in anything other than Chinese was very difficult, especially with customers, yet The Daughter still insisted I help out selling items and dealing with prospective buyers. She knew I had trouble with this. When I stumbled over a word or opted to simply nod, she was NOT happy and would scold me and say, "You are so stupid! Are you deaf?! What is wrong with you that you cannot speak even a few words?! Who could want you? Ayye…Stupid girl!" I was always cut to the heart with such words. I wanted to do well. Was I really so stupid? Tears would fill my eyes. Why couldn't they be happy with me? I never realized that a few people who saw this would share it with Judy.

Friendly Curiosity

What one person views as a curse can be a tremendous blessing to another. "Ahh…that Judy! Who does she think she is? She talks so much…that's why she sells so little!" The Daughter said one day. Of course I heard what she said. When I wasn't bringing in goods from the back room, sweeping and cleaning, I was sitting with The Old Lady, softly patting her hand or back as she sat in a chair set up where she could watch all the people, coming and going. When she grew tired I would take her to the back to watch TV. As I listened to The Daughter complain I thought, "How fortunate for me that Judy loves to talk to everyone. She talks to me, too." A hint of a smile formed in the corners of my lips as I thought this thought. "What are you smiling about?" The Daughter snapped at me. I hadn't realized that the thoughts about my new friend had shown on my face. I said nothing. But I continued to smile, patting The Old Lady's arm thinking about my new friend.

Judy's friendly demeanor opened doors as well. She began conversations with so many people working around me that she began to hear the truth about my situation. At first she was completely shocked and couldn't believe that I was not free to go wherever I pleased. For the first time she began to watch

The Old Lady, her Daughter, and me carefully. She was told The Daughter often shouted at me and called me names, but because she didn't understand Mandarin, she had no idea. She watched my behavior around The Old Lady. "No, this couldn't be right…Sharon is just being sweet and caring for her grandmother," she thought. But my 'grandmother' never smiled at me; never gave me a hug or kiss; never spoke my name. She began to notice how I was treated by The Old Lady's Daughter. Short, sharp commands always; I was never given a break; I was always doing the hardest tasks; I never laughed or smiled. Something wasn't right. How long could this talkative lady keep her mouth shut?

I am sure there were others who thought that things were not quite right with the relationship I had with The Old Lady and her Daughter. I was treated harshly and scolded so often that if I had been simply an employee, I would've quit. But day after day I was there, hustling to work hard while they barked commands at me. "No, something was just not right," Judy thought. It was this suspicion that lead Judy to start asking deeper questions to others that worked in the flea mart.

Another lady, Marie, had noticed the strange behaviors as well. "I cannot get involved because the family knows me too well, but I want to give you some money for the young girl (of course, meaning me) to help her in some way," Marie told Judy one day. I had no idea any of this was going on. So many times I longed for someone to help, to notice, to at least acknowledge my plight, but no one ever did. I had pretty much given up that idea.

Building Trust

Judy and I continued our friendship secretly. I would walk past her booth slowly and we'd exchange smiles or a word or two. This went on for nearly a year before I felt I could truly trust her.

"Sharon, this is not right. They don't treat you like a human being. It's not right." Judy said to me one day after she'd learned about my situation. "Why don't you call the police?" "I'm scared. Where I go?" I said. "Where I gonna go?" I was fearful of what would happen to me. I thought I would just be brought back to them and things we become unbearable. I was so fearful. This was my family. What could I do? "I will help you," she said. At that moment I knew I could trust her.

The Wrong Meat

I have mentioned how I hated shopping with The Daughter, but if she wanted me to go I had to. There were a very few times she couldn't go with me and I was sent with the grandson's girlfriend or someone else. I was told what to get and given a list. How on earth could I read this list? I did my best to memorize all of the items on it. I pushed the cart around the store and collected all of the items. There was one, though, a cut of beef that I was not familiar with. I stopped for quite a while at the meat section trying desperately to read the labels. I finally had to take a guess and picked up the large plastic wrapped bundle and put it in the cart.

"What?! What is this?!" The Daughter shouted. "I cannot use this for our supper—it is not the right meat! What is wrong with you, you stupid girl! I gave you a list and told you everything I needed!" She began to scream and curse and eventually her mother, The Old Lady got involved. "I told you she was worthless! And this piece of meat is more expensive," she said, looking at the receipt. "I see what you are trying to do, you thief!" Since we had been in America some of the more violent attacks from The Old Lady had lessened when others were in the house, so I was taken completely by surprise when she suddenly kicked me and then reached out and grabbed my hair, like she had done in Taiwan. She started to drag me like she had done before, but she was too old and I was much stronger. I yelled so loud she let go, thinking her daughter's husband might hear. I ran down the hall to the bathroom and locked myself in. I was breathing heavy and crying hard. My neck hurt and I was already having trouble with my back constantly aching. I was concerned permanent damage had been done already. Something broke in me. I knew something had to change. "This is it!" I said to myself. "I can't do this…I can't anymore…I just can't…"

The Phone Number

The next day, sore, I returned with The Old Lady and her Daughter to the shop. Judy had been renting her spot in the shop for nearly a year, but with Darrin being sick and her being advanced in years, she knew that her time working like this was at its end. She thought about me a lot and realized that others around me might not be as bold as she had been towards me and she felt she couldn't so easily abandon me without some thread for me to hang on to. She decided to give me her phone number before she left. She found the back of a receipt and tore a small corner from it. Purposely writing as clearly as possible each number for me to read, she folded the small strip of paper and hid it in her hand. She made her rounds, as she usually did, greeting the others, chatting a bit here and there in the harmlessly flirty way she had. I saw her move closer and closer to where I was working. She always had a smile and a cheery comment for me, sometimes a wink and even blowing a few kisses in my direction. I loved this woman. I felt human around her. This time as she came to greet me she reached out her hand, carefully grabbing my own in hers. I felt something in her grip. It wrinkled slightly and I grasped it subconsciously. I dared not look at what was now balled up in my hand. "If you need *anything*—call me; be careful," she whispered, acting as if she had asked me something else so no one would know. "Goodbye…" I nodded and smiled and pulled my hand back with the small wadded up piece of paper and placed it in my pocket.

The Plan

The horror of the previous night stayed with me and I had decided what I needed to do. Now I had a connection and a phone number to help me out of this prison.

There were no windows in the storeroom in the back of the shop and it was pretty much ignored by everyone. Because the bathroom was there, I had a good reason why I might be back there from time to time without being afraid of getting in trouble. I knew I could use the phone in there without anyone knowing. I could never use the phone at home. I was watched like a hawk.

My opportunity came one Thursday. The Old Lady and her Daughter had made an appointment to get their hair done together. The family had a girl who kept an eye on me from time to time and there were also cameras everywhere. I had a short window of time that I could go to the workshop and use the phone to call Judy to let her know what time I planned to leave. Tonight was the night. I felt I had just one chance and this was it.

I walked to the workshop, opened the door and slowly walked in. I picked up the phone. My heart was beating so loud I thought it would jump right out of my chest! I took a deep breath, unfolded my precious scrap of paper and dialed the numbers. "Hello. Judy?" I said cautiously. "This Sharon; I ok, need help to leave." I continued to try to tell of my plan in broken English. I was only hoping she understood what I needed and was still willing to help.

"You must call the police," Judy instructed after I had told her my plan to escape. "I am not sure what to do..." her voice trailed off and I heard her talking to her husband. The words were muffled but then Judy's voice returned to the phone, strong and clear. "Ok…I can come pick you up. Tell me when and where."

This was it, REALLY it. I had never thought about running away before…where would I go? Now I had some place, even if it was for a short time. I would at least be away from this family and the hate and abuse. Determination filled me as my hand shook, the phone still held to my ear. I spoke with confidence as I told Judy the address, making sure she understood, I repeated it again. Then I finished by saying,

"7:30 p.m. Thursday night. Come that time. I outside. I ready."

Chapter 13

The Escape

My heart was pounding so loud I could feel the blood pulsing in my ears. Every nerve in my body was on alert. Did I hear someone behind me? My toes were wet and cold and bits green grass stuck between them. I hardly noticed the water that puddled at my feet. I mechanically moved the end of the hose back and forth. "Keep watering the grass and flowers. No one must suspect a thing," I nervously commanded myself. The slow rushing of the water from the hose, the nightly sounds on the block were forced into the distant background as my eyes nervously darted up and down the street, searching for the car that belonged to my savior, Judy, who I knew would soon be here.

I had rolled the garbage cans to the curb and began to water the grass, like I did every Thursday night, the only task I did unattended, a brief moment away from the watchful eyes of my captors. It was a typical warm August night in 2005. I wore the same dirty green shorts, paper thin from being worn day after day and a dingy white blouse dotted with brown flowers that hung oddly over my boney frame. I had taken off my sandals to keep them from getting wet as I stood now, in the middle of the front lawn, trying hard not to shake from the exhilarating fear and anticipation that gripped my entire body.

I took a deep breath. The puddle at my feet grew larger and a small snakelike stream of water slowly crept forward, reaching the sidewalk. How long could I stand out here without being called back into that house, that suffocating prison of mine? A car rolled slowly down the street. Could it be? It continued past me only to pull into a driveway at the far end of the block. Thump, thump, thump, the blood continued to pulse, this time I felt it on the sides of my head, keeping time—as the slow, painful seconds dragged on and on with no relief. I absent-mindedly wiggled my toes as the water poured over them. Tonight *had* to be the night. It had to! My thoughts trailed back to the night before as I helped The Old Lady take her bath and then massaged her feet until she fell asleep. I had soothed her late into the night, as I usually did, until deep sleep fell over her and it was well past midnight.

Goodbye, 'Grandma'

The Old Lady lay there asleep. I looked at her face—how old she had become yet still her skin was soft and youthful. I continued to pat her hand, it was so automatic now; I did it without thinking. I knew what I had to do next. I took a deep breath and bent my knee next to her and quietly said, "Grandma, I wish you had treated me right, like a real granddaughter. You told everyone I was your granddaughter, but I am not. I just wanted to be treated like a person, a human being. I wish I could go back in time and change things, but I cannot. I would never leave you in this way, by running away. I would have appreciated you for the rest of my life if you had only shown me some respect, but you did not; you treated me shamefully as a slave. I cannot serve you or help you anymore."

I whispered all this to her, her heavy breathing drowning out most of my words. "Why wouldn't you accept me? Why couldn't you love me? I tried so hard to please you and love you in return. Why couldn't I be good enough for you? But I must go. I have to go..." My confession ended with, "I'm sorry..." I was surprised to feel a small tear roll to the edge of my nose and slowly fall onto my knee. Physically and emotionally drained, I lay down on the floor near the Old Lady's bed and covered myself with a single tattered dirty blanket. Cupping my hands together for a pillow, I fell asleep. When I awoke the next day, I knew it would be my last with this 'family' of mine.

Suddenly, I was snapped back into the moment as I noticed a long dark sedan cruise by the house. Wait. I had seen this same car before; this was the second time it circled past me. It continued down the street and turned to make its third pass, hoping the street was clear and that I had seen it. It was her. I knew it had to be her! The pounding of my heart grew so loud I could no longer distinguish it from the other sounds around me. My body felt heavy and tense. I thought I might jump right out of my skin if I had to wait a second longer. The car I had eyed rolled to a stop at the end of the street, its brake lights giving me a gentle wink—"You know it's time; I am here to take you away from all this." For a moment I was frozen. I told my feet to run but nothing happened. The opportunity to leave this horrid life was shouting at me and incredibly I was too paralyzed to take it. What was I waiting for?

Like a gunshot signifying the beginning of a great race, I bolted, dropping the hose, running as fast as I could towards the end of the street and that dark silent sedan that was patiently waiting for me. Everything I owned left behind, except my tattered shirt and pants that didn't quite fit right, the clothes, reminding me of the life I had been living these past twenty years, a torn and ravaged life. In my bare wet feet I ran in fear. I was sure that someone was chasing me, an arm reaching out to grab me. I did not dare look back. Would I reach the car in time? I felt the warm rough pavement tearing at the bottoms of my feet, threatening to slow me down. How far that distance to the end of the block seemed to be to me! It went on forever. I reached the handle on the back door and jerked it open. I jumped in to the back seat of the car pulling the door shut behind me. Without a sound we sped on as if nothing had happened. Gasping for air, my heart still pounding, my ears pulsing, I felt lightheaded. I fearfully looked back through the small tinted window. No one. It was quiet and still and dark. I continued to look back in disbelief. The summer sky had made this night glow, a deep royal blue, perfect, beautiful. Did I really just do this? My breathing was heavy and my hands shook uncontrollably. I felt a slight sickening feeling in my stomach, hoping this was not all some dream. When I could no longer see the house or even a glimpse of the street that had kept me in bondage, I finally turned away to see where I was headed. As for my sleeping captors and the upscale neighborhood they lived in it was just another Thursday night.

Although Judy and her husband, Darrin—not yet realizing the true scope of this rescue—were calm, my head was still spinning from my grand escape. "Dink, dink, dink, dink," the sedan signaled as we drove up the ramp onto the freeway. After some time, we made our way closer to their quiet secluded house near the beach. "You must be hungry. Let's stop and pick up something. How about some burgers?" Judy suggested. I had eaten a hamburger only once before. Several of The Old Lady's grandchildren had picked some up and in a forgetful moment, offered me one. It had been a wonderful treat from the usual soured leftovers. The car heaved and bumped as we pulled up into the parking lot. The neon yellow and red of the sign of the restaurant was oddly comforting. Even though I continued to insist that I wasn't a bit hungry, I managed to eat the entire burger, fries and extra-large shake we got before we eventually made it to her front door.

My New Home

Judy's house was beautiful! She led me upstairs and told me to relax and get cleaned up. I had forgotten that I was still barefoot and small blades of grass and bits of dirt clung to my feet, legs and ankles. "If you'd like, you can take a shower. Use whatever soaps and shampoos you find," her soothing voice offered me such peace and comfort. Use whatever soaps and shampoos I could find? I was never allowed to use anything but dish soap on myself and a shower with clean running water was out of the question. I took a long hot shower. Scented soap, floral shampoo…I rubbed it over every inch of me. It felt good. I let the wonderful pure water pour over me for a long time. I hadn't felt this clean in such a very long time. I stepped out of the shower and dried myself with large soft towel that lay folded on the counter, placed there for me. The energy and adrenaline that had gotten me to this place began to fade and suddenly I felt very tired. It was late and my body was telling me that I ran a marathon today. I had been running a lot longer than that most of my life. I wanted to relax, just sleep, but my mind was still geared up and the fear and anxiety of being found out and sent back to that place—to those people—kept nagging at me.

A Bed of My Own

I think Judy could see that I was exhausted and a good night's sleep would be best for all of us, so she led me upstairs into her guest bedroom. A room to myself was incredible enough, but a bed to sleep in…and all to myself? I felt like I had gone to Heaven. Clean blankets and pillows and a comforter covered in the most beautiful flower pattern spilled over the bed, its colors matching the walls and carpet, and the room was filled with gorgeous smells! Judy hastily found something I could sleep in...a far cry from what I was used to...and apologized for its size and promised we would shop for something proper the next day. In my broken English and tearful gratitude I thanked her over and over, but she would have none of it. "Nonsense!" she replied. "You go to sleep and we'll do this clothes thing proper in the morning." As I lay there in the bed I stretched out my arms. I felt soft fluffy bed on either side, without end. I rolled to the right and then to the left. Still the bed continued. I felt overwhelmed inside at the day's events. "God, I thank you so much for helping me, for bringing Judy to me to help me. Please, help me tomorrow to face what may come." Emotions and thoughts swirled around in my head for quite a while as I lay there waiting for sleep to come. It did and it stayed. The sun came up and I was still asleep. Something that I could never remember ever happening to me before...I stayed in bed until I wanted to get up.

Like a Princess

Judy was an amazing yet eccentric older woman. Her sense of style was incredible. She wasted no time in taking me to the mall for clothes shopping. Her specialty: shoes! My whole body tingled with excitement and delight as we pulled up to one of the biggest malls in the state. I had never seen such a place! Shop after shop of clothes, shoes, purses and accessories filled my eyes. Then we walked in to Nordstrom. Oh my! I had never seen such beautiful things. "First thing is to get some shoes for you..." Judy said in such a serious tone.

It was as if she was on a mission to erase every part of that downtrodden slave that I had been. "What size do you wear?" she casually tossed her words my way, but they hit me like a bowling ball. What size *did* I wear? I had no idea. I felt my face begin to burn as embarrassment slowly filled my cheeks. All of my clothes and shoes had been given to me by others and never fit me quite right. I wore them until they were either too tight to put on or they were falling apart from daily wear. What size did I wear? A lump formed in my throat as I meekly said, "I...I not know...I never buy shoe..." My voice trailed off hoping Judy would understand. Like a machine she continued to scan the merchandize, not phased a bit by my astonishing revelation. "Ohh...yes, these ones...try these on." She handed me the first pair of brand-new shoes I had ever held in my hands. The shoes were light silver in color with a thin strap across the back, allowing the back of the heel to show. The straps wove around in a herringbone pattern to the front of the shoe and then tied in a neat bow with the ends slightly dangling down the sides, highlighting the toe of the shoe which looked a ballerina's slipper. I fell in love with these shoes! As I slipped my bare calloused feet inside, I felt like Cinderella...no longer among the ashes. Hope that a princess was inside of me became all too possible. Although the pair were flats, I walked around in them rather awkwardly, never having walked in any type of heel before. I had no time to get use to them, however, because we were on to the next purchase and the next. There was no other way to describe it: It was a feast of shopping!

I believe that Judy was just as excited to shop for me as I was to receive her wonderful gifts. She spared no expense on herself and she extended that to me. I had somehow stumbled across a savior of sorts in this wonderful woman, and I would forever be grateful to her and the kindness she poured upon me.

I was so caught up in my first day of freedom that I never thought about what might be happening back at the house with The Old Lady and her Daughter. My loyalty and total surrender to their daily demands had kept them from ever thinking that I might have run away or escaped. They were sure I had been kidnapped or somehow had become lost. With no sign of me in the house that night, they called the police and made a full report.

'Sharon' Is Missing

"I was upstairs, taking a nap, I guess, when I awoke suddenly and called for Sharon." The Old Lady's Daughter told the police officers who had just arrived at the house. They were responding to the call of a missing person. "I hurried downstairs and began to search the house; I looked everywhere, calling her name, but when I couldn't find her, I called my husband to see if he had seen Sharon."

"I had been working on some paperwork for my business when I heard Sharon outside, dragging the trash cans around to the backyard. She is so small, you know, she has a hard time managing them," he went on. "I tell her to leave them, it's ok, I can handle them," he continued, adding a few lies to his story. Offer me help? There were much harder chores than this I did completely on my own, even when I was sick. I got no help then. "I don't remember hearing her come back in. It wasn't until my wife was asking me where Sharon was that I had remembered hearing her outside." He explained. "It was around…," His wife cut in then, "Sharon waters the lawn and brings the trashcans in from the street every Thursday. She always comes in after that. It's just not like her—I don't understand—I went outside and saw the hose laying on the ground, water still gushing from the end, and a pair of shoes left on the lawn. I became worried and sent my husband to search for her." The older man cleared his throat and began again, "I decided to walk through the neighborhood and down towards the school, thinking she may have gotten lost. I asked everyone I saw if they had seen her, but no one had. I walked slowly through the park but saw nothing. It was as if she vanished into thin air." The police continued to ask question after question, hoping to find a clue. "Did she go out or perhaps driven somewhere?" "She doesn't drive or go anywhere alone," was the reply. "What about her friends? Maybe she is with them," the officers inquired further. "She has no…, not many friends…" was the answer.

Every question led to a dead end. Sharon goes nowhere. Sharon has no friends. Sharon doesn't drive. The picture painted of me was an odd one. Maybe I was a mentally or emotionally stunted young woman in their eyes…I don't think the thought occurred to them that I was a slave living in this wealthy community and had finally seen a window of opportunity to escape my personal hell.

The officers began canvassing the neighborhood, interviewing everyone. They even interviewed the family pastor. Interview after interview revealed nothing. Sharon was missing and those around her seemed to know nothing about her at all.

On the News

The unusual news that a small Asian woman, perhaps mentally impaired, was wandering lost or possibly abducted in a rather affluent town, became the headline of the local news and suddenly a picture of me was seen all over the television. It didn't occur to me that people may have seen both me and Judy shopping and it looked suspicious. A woman who had seen that report on the news began to follow us from store to store. As we carried our treasures to the car, the woman wrote down our license plate number and contacted the police.

"On August 18, 2005 at approximately 9 p.m., local resident Sharon [Ho] was reported missing from her residential area...Anyone with information regarding this matter is asked to call the local police department."

—Official Police Report, August, 2005

I hadn't a clue local news had shown a photo of me as a missing person and that a manhunt had already started. Judy's husband, after seeing the report himself, worried he could be getting mixed up in something he might not have all the facts to, had also called the police himself. When I arrived back at Judy's house, I had no idea that right after unpacking all my brand-new clothes, two officers would be at the door, inquiring about me and hoping to get to the bottom of things. This would soon lead to a house full of enforcement agents, all trying to piece together what could be an 'international' incident.

"Based on a tip received from a citizen who recognized Ms. [Ho] from television media coverage. Police detectives, assisted by members of the Sheriff's Department, have located Ms. [Ho] on the evening of August 19, 2015."

—Official Police Report, August, 2005

"Can we please speak to Ms. Ho," the uniformed men asked as Darrin answered the door. "The police are here?" Judy said as she heard the discussion from upstairs. I was so scared I didn't know what to do. She joined her husband and the officers at the door, but I panicked. I couldn't go back to The Old Lady. I was so overcome by such a powerful fear that I hid in one of the closets. When the officers and Judy and Darrin came looking for me, I was so frightened I refused to come out. After a time of pleading, promising me that everything would be alright, I cautiously came out and threw myself at the feet of a young officer.

Please...No Send Me Back!

I fell to my knees, clinging to his ankles, begging him not to send me back to such a horrible place. Tears streamed down my face as I managed to choke out in broken English, pleading, "Please, no send me back...please!...I no go back—it be bad for me to go back...please, no..." I broke down in a puddle on the floor, sobbing, grasping his pant legs. I don't think he knew what to do. Stunned, I heard him mutter under his breath, "What the...?" I think he was just as overcome as I was because slowly he knelt down next to me, his face filled with compassion, and promised me he wouldn't send me anywhere I didn't want to go. "It's gonna be ok," he calmly repeated over and over to me. "I am not taking you anywhere..." In moments the house filled with more officers of all kinds and I overheard a radio call to have a translator sent in to help. I was led to the table in the kitchen where I sat down and began my best to tell my story and was told the 'family' was looking for me. I had been reported as a missing person. Judy set a hot cup of tea in front of me and began taking coffee orders from all who wanted some. The translator arrived as well, a tall handsome young man, who had the kindest eyes. He began trying several languages, Cantonese, Mandarin, until I replied, "Yes, I understand..." I wiped my face on a napkin and a warm feeling of safety fell over me.

It took quite some time to unravel the details of what had happened, why I had left The Old Lady and her Daughter. The officers wrote down every detail as the investigation went very late into the night...

*"...So far, our investigation has revealed that
[said person] left her home of her own free
will and accord and is in good health. Police
detectives are continuing to investigate this
matter. Based on the continuing investigation
and upon the wishes of Ms. [Ho], no further
information relating to the reason for her
leaving, her current location or any other
information will be released at this time.*

*The important information is that Ms. [Ho] left
her residence of her own volition and that she
has been located and is safe."*

—Official Police Report, August, 2005

The Search Warrant

The information that I gave to the police officers that night
set off all kinds of red flags about why I had left and what was
going on back at The Daughter's house. There was plenty of
suspicion that I was a victim of human trafficking and that my
'family' was somehow involved. The case was referred to the
Human Trafficking Division of Homeland Security Investigations. A search warrant was needed so evidence could be collected. This assignment had reached a young Homeland Security Special Agent who had to write an affidavit in support
of a search warrant and then get it signed by a federal judge
quickly. It was Sunday and the agent learned that the judge
was at a local amusement park with his family on his day off.

"What?!" the agent said as he put the papers in a folder and headed to his car. "I gotta find this judge by checking every ride and show in the park? Well, I wish I had time for a roller-coaster ride or two myself." As he clipped the seatbelt around his waist and started the engine, his partner jumped in and shut the door. "Never a dull moment, huh?" he commented as they pulled out and onto the street. This agent would become such a blessing to me; always fighting for me. He would make sure he kept in touch with me through the years, always hoping things would work out for me and that life would be better.

A team of Homeland Security special agents, all wearing tactical gear, showed up at the house of The Daughter, her husband and The Old Lady. The warrant was given to them to read. I am sure they were all pretty scared, not knowing what was happening. The agents split up and began to search every inch of the house. One by one everyone in the house was questioned separately. Both The Daughter and her husband refused to say a word, but not The Old Lady. As she answered each question more and more details came to light about what my life was like and how I came to live with her. I had never been separated from The Old Lady in all the years I had lived with her. If there was anyone who knew all the answers, it was her. In her truthfulness she never realized she had provided key information to the agents that would later help me a great deal. The house was searched, computers seized, and interviews conducted, including several neighbors. All of this was just the beginning of my struggle to stay free, which would take many twist and turns and force the secrets this family held about me out into the open. I would have many lawyers, police officers and federal agents, case workers and countless others taking up my cause and it would take a few years, eventually thrusting me back to face that family but for now, I was free and just beginning to understand the challenges of living free.

Chapter 14

Sharon No Longer

If there was one good thing that I learned from all those years of serving the Old Lady, it was an appreciation for well-made clothes, clothes that had a lot of style and fashion. Day after day, since I was barely big enough to reach the hangers, I had laid out her beautifully tailor-made clothes, her colorful silks and furs, hand-stitched by the finest Chinese clothing makers. I had a natural gift, I guess, at putting colors and styles together and I enjoyed doing it. But now living with Judy, a well-off stylish woman herself, I was bound to go shopping at some point, and shopping we went!

You may have heard of stories of people who were lost in the desert, starving and near dying of thirst. When they finally are rescued, they have to be very careful not to allow themselves to gorge on food and water too soon, for it could be very damaging to their health. Though the lack of money held me back somewhat, I was that person, starved inside, but now I was in heaven as we hit store after store and I enjoyed every minute of it! It was strange for me to think that just weeks before I was waiting on that family every minute in my tattered old clothes, hoping for enough to eat and now I was treated like a princess—"What do you need? What would you like for breakfast? What shop should we go in next?" Judy would ask. It was so unreal to me.

My New Routine

Every morning Judy let me sleep late. *Every day* until after 10 a.m.! I'd hear her say to her husband, "Let her sleep. She needs her rest." She cooked breakfast for me, washed my clothes—every day. She became like a mother to me. I will never forget this—being truly treated like a daughter. I was loved by her. I started calling her 'Mom.'

Sharon No Longer

It was Judy who suggested I change my name. "You told me that The Old Lady gave you the name, 'Sharon'? Judy asked me one day. "Well, you are not her slave anymore, why keep that name?" I thought this was a pretty good idea so I responded with, "What name, Mom, you want?" Putting her hand on her chin she looked at me with a sparkle in her eye and said, "I like Shari. What do you think?" "Yes, Mom, I now Shari." I gave her a hug and we both laughed together.

The HTTF

The Human Trafficking Task Force (HTTF) is an incredible organization.

It is a collaboration of law enforcement, victim service providers, non-profit organizations, faith-based organizations, government entities and the community. Its mission is to work together, taking a victim-centered approach with the common goal of combating human trafficking and related crimes.

Among the organizations that make up the HTTF are local Police Departments and Community Service Programs, the Highway Patrol, District Attorney's Office, the local Sheriff's Department, The Salvation Army, Department of Homeland Security, and various non-profit organizations. Collaboratively, with over 60 organizations to close gaps in services, they assist victims of human trafficking.

Since 2004, the HTTF has assisted over 500 victims of human trafficking from 36 countries, with the majority from the United States. It had only been operating for a little more than a year when I escaped The Old Lady in 2005.

It was the HTTF that brought Amy Henry into my life.

My First Case Manager

Three days after I had escaped from The Old Lady and her Daughter, I was connected with the Human Trafficking Task

Force. When the police had come to Judy's house that night, CSP, Victim Assistance Program, had contacted Amy Henry and arranged for me to meet with her. Human trafficking victims were assigned a case manager to see that work visas, green cards, housing—any immediate needs—were dealt with so human trafficking survivors, such as myself, could transition into a more 'normal' way of life. Amy Henry was my first case manager. Amy had been working with The Cambodian Family with the Partnership for Trafficking Victim Services, working specifically with foreign national victims of trafficking and was an HTTF founding member. I was so scared and nervous at the time. I could barely speak English and felt safe at Judy's house and wasn't sure what was going to happen next.

"Shari," Judy called to me from downstairs. "I want to talk to you about something," her voice trailed off as I made my way down the stairs into the kitchen. "The Victim Witness Program has case workers who are assigned to people who have gone through what you have gone through. Why don't we see how they can help? We have an appointment to meet with case manager Amy Henry tomorrow. I'll be there with you. We'll eat lunch and just talk about how you can get help to live so you won't ever have to worry about The Old Lady or her Daughter again."

I trusted Judy. She had been the only one to see what was going on in my life and had cared enough to reach out to me. I was free because of her. "Okay, I go…" I replied, still feeling a bit nervous. The next day we drove to the restaurant where we were to meet Amy. "I thought meeting here might be a little less stressful than in some stuffy office," Judy explained as the waitress led us to a spacious table near the back. "Thank you, we are expecting a friend to join us." Menus were passed out and drink orders were taken. This was a strange world to me. I was not allowed to eat out with The Old Lady and her Daughter. If I wasn't cooking for them at home, they usually had me pick up food they had ordered, but here I was, sitting in a restaurant like everyone else, given a menu and being waited on for the first time. My nerves gave way to the joy I felt at being treated like a normal human being.

Amy Henry

"Hi. I'm Amy Henry." A voice suddenly spoke from behind me. "You must be Judy? And are you Shari?" We all shook hands and she sat down across from me. "I had heard about your story and want to tell you how brave I think you were to have escaped the way you did. You don't have to worry. You will NEVER have to go back with that family." She assured me. "I want you to know that I am here to help you and get you all the assistance you need—any paperwork, money, a place to stay—anything that you might need. I know you don't really know me right now, but I hope you come to trust me. I am here to help you. I really am." Amy went on to encourage me and reassure me that everything was going to be okay. Our meeting was not a very long one, but Amy asked if she could come by Judy's house in a day or two to talk more. I felt good inside. I was still unsure about all that was happening around me, but something inside said it was all going to be okay. I guess I believed Amy at that moment. This was the good day I was looking for in all my bad days. All the nights I spent telling myself tomorrow would be better, maybe, finally, those days had come.

Since 2003, Amy had worked with foreign-born women (and men) who had been freed from forced sexual exploitation and forced labor, and were rebuilding their lives. As part of the HTTF, Amy worked with other professionals to identify and care for victims of trafficking and to build a network of social service providers, legal entities, ethnic community groups and faith-based groups who were willing to care for victims and prevent trafficking from happening in their own community. Amy was also a regular speaker, speaking about modern day slavery and providing assistance to organizations who would like to help survivors of human trafficking. Amy loved working with the faith-based community groups and later introduced me to The Salvation Army. This was Amy's passion, which has led her to travel to over 28 countries.

Amy kept her promise and came to visit me a day or two later. We talked about a lot of things during that second meeting. I led her upstairs to show her my room. "This where I hide—police come to house, but I so scared," I said, opening the closet door. I began to feel more comfortable with this case manager. Soon I was showing her my new shoes, the ones Judy had bought me that first night I had run away. I was so excited. I just talked and talked! Amy thought my shoes were so cute. "I love the color! They look like the shoes of a princess." She said. This was the beginning of one of the most important relationships I would have in my life. I would rely on this new friend for over a year and a half and it would be Amy Henry that would eventually travel with me to one more country to add to her list—my native Taiwan.

Many Things to Learn

"Do you know how to count?" Amy asked me one day. Part of Amy's job was to teach me the skills I needed to be independent. I thought about her question and remembered my mom asking that same thing, "…count ten days…I will come back for you." She'd said. Then I said to Amy, "Yeah…when I little…ah, yeah," I kept that old thought to myself. I knew I needed to count more numbers than up to ten, "I learn…" I responded.

"Okay, we are going to learn how to shop and use money, so let's start with twenty dollars," Amy explained. "Have you been grocery shopping before?" I had many times with The Old Lady and her Daughter, but I never paid for anything or picked out things other than what they told me to pick. "Let's say we take a walk to the store and buy some things?" Amy suggested. When we reached the market we went inside and looked around a bit. "What kinds of things do you like to eat? We can start with some basics." Amy instructed. "Let's get a cart, look at the prices and see what we can get with $20." At first Amy just walked with me letting me look and pick things out, but I found this very hard to do. After quite a while I had only picked two things and was becoming frustrated. "Wow, maybe I set the goal a little too high today," Amy said, a bit shocked at my struggle. "I'll help this time." So we went to the produce section and picked out some vegetables and fruit and then moved on to bread. We talked about the prices as Amy pointed out the signs, things sold by the pound were weighed on a scale; other items were priced as marked. It was a lot to remember, but Amy reminded me this was only our first trip. Then we stood in line and she showed me how to pay for it. I was grateful Amy didn't embarrass me. I was an adult and very conscience of the fact I didn't know things that even little kids already knew.

More Lessons

"I brought the ads with me today, "Amy said as she walked in the door. "We're gonna practice looking at the store ads, finding things you want to buy, adding them up and then sub-tracting them from $10, okay?" she explained as she opened the paper and smoothed it out on the table. We spent hours doing this. It was kind of fun and less stressful than facing a person in the market. I got pretty good at what things I might want and knowing change for a $10 dollar bill.

Becoming More Independent

I remember my first time at Mother's Market after I had escaped. I ordered the same things The Daughter had always ordered for her and her mother. I ate it all myself! It felt so good…bread, a sandwich, spinach, tofu, fish, cheese and a pickle...I think it cost like $12.00. I gave them a $20 and got $8.00 back!

When I went to stores and places to buy things, it was always with Amy or Judy and later, by myself. In all those times I can't remember anyone ever cheating me out of change. Many times I didn't know how to add prices properly. The first time I went all by myself I got so frustrated and embarrassed, I walked out. I cried when I got outside the door. Usually people were always helpful when they saw that I struggled.

Money

Early on, my case manager would reimburse Judy for the cost of whatever supplies I needed. One of the first things I bought was a phone. It was Amy who came with me. "A phone is very important to have. You'll need it a lot." She said. There were contracts to sign and I was glad she was there to help explain it all to me.

Judy loved to shop and we enjoyed doing this together. We'd shop and laugh and have such fun. I was excited every time we'd go out. I *wanted* to buy—especially shoes. I LOVE shoes! I didn't know what the styles were at that time, just whether I thought they looked good on me. I didn't know what size I was so I just tried them all on. When it came to shoes and pants, I always had to try them on. I was a size zero at that time! Pants were always too long and I would go to the kids section in order to find something that would be the right length. I really like soft materials, but never really liked jeans.

I would have my clothes altered because it was cheaper back then. Clothes could be expensive and when I was shopping with Judy we went to Nordstrom and other high-end stores.

Ross

Then I found Ross. It was love at first sight! I remember when I felt confident enough to go to Ross all by myself. I always paid with a $10 dollar bill. I looked at the price and knew what $6-$7 was and what the change would be; I knew how to count to 10. Using a $20 was still hard for me. But I knew 1, 2, 3, 4…not really much more after that.

I bought a lot of clothes when I shopped. I guess I had to make up for all the ones I didn't have. As a slave, the colors I wore were mostly blue or pink or crazy bright like orange or red. I now felt drawn to black and grey as colors. I don't know why. I loved black then, when I was first set free. I like colors now. I buy more colorful ones, my favorite color being green. I really didn't know how to budget in those days so clothes were always first on my shopping list.

Mio

I walked just about everywhere I went, but in the U.S., people drive everywhere. If you don't have a license, then public transportation is a must. My next lesson was learning to ride the bus. There were so many wonderful people I met through the HTTF. One of those new friends was Mio, a young Japanese graduate student who helped me with life skills, and riding the bus was one of those skills.

Mio spent days mapping out a route, even wait times at the bus stop. Then she rode the route herself, to make sure everything would go smoothly. This was a 3-mile trip, but my first, and Mio wanted it to be a success. "Okay, we'll ride it together and then you'll be ready for your first trip alone. Don't worry…I'll follow behind you in the car." She said with a smile. We stood at the bus stop and the bus pulled up and I boarded. I dropped the coins in the slot and found a seat near a window as the bus pulled away. Mio pulled away, too, and followed the bus. She knew which way the bus was going and as it stopped, she stopped and waited for it to continue its route. The driver of the bus saw Mio in the rearview mirror, following closely. When he stopped, she stopped. This was beginning to concern him. The route he was supposed to take was a straight line, but he abruptly changed as he turned left, then right, trying to shake this car that had been following him. Mio was confused at why the driver didn't follow his route, but she had no way to tell the driver what she was doing, so she just kept following. Suddenly the bus came to a halt and the driver jumped out and began yelling at Mio. She was able to explain to him what was happening. "My friend is on the bus—I just wanted to make sure she was okay." The bus driver laughed, "I was going to call the cops on you!" We both had a good laugh about that!

Mio didn't give up on me and continued to tutor me, even helping me to study to get a learner's permit to drive. She'd visit restaurants and write out whole menus for me to practice with so when I went out I could order. She worked with me for four years. She was such a good friend!

My First Job

I was determined to work for myself and earn my own money. As grateful I was for Judy's help and her kindness in letting me live with her, I knew to really be free I had to provide for myself, and that meant a job. I had been living at Judy's for close to nine months now. It was sad to have to leave, but it was time to move on.

"Mom, it so hard, I leave. I so thankful for all you done. I miss you." I said as we tearfully hugged goodbye. But both of us knew this was the right thing to do. Judy had a friend who was willing to have me move in with her. Her name was Elsa. Her children had left home, all but her son, and she had an extra room she said I could stay in. She had a large house and yard with a large dog. I had met this woman briefly when I was still living with The Old Lady and her Daughter; she had walked in to the shop with Judy while I was working one day. She seemed kind and although at that time she didn't know my story, she was now very sympathetic to my situation. She had a housekeeper of her own, but I often helped out with chores around the house, cooking for her son and walking the dog. I decided to live with Elsa, get a job and save enough money to live on my own. Elsa lived within walking distance to many job opportunities so this seemed like a good plan.

Amy and others at the HTTF had worked hard and fast to get the paperwork in motion for me to have the proper documents to work and to stay in the U.S. That is when I found a preschool very close to Elsa's house that offered me a job working with toddlers. I spoke little English, and my job skills were limited. I even needed help filling out the job application! But I knew I was a hard worker and a very fast learner. They hired me, paying me minimum wage. I would be paid every two weeks.

My First Paycheck

I was so excited to get that first paycheck. I had to ask Elsa, "How much this?"

"Its 500 dollars," she said, which seemed like a fortune to me at the time. "I rich!" I excitedly told her. She shook her head and laughed. I decided to save as much of the money as I could because I didn't have to pay her rent at that time. She talked me into going to the bank to open an account.

"What do you mean, she can't open a savings account?" Elsa said astonishingly to the bank clerk. "I'm very sorry, but you must have a second form of identification—just a work I.D. won't do." the teller said apologetically. "Well, we'll try someplace else, I guess," So we went to several other banks in the area but found the same problem. Then we walked into Union Bank. They were wonderful! It was the only bank to accept me so I could cash my check. I was nervous every single time I went to the bank. I brought extra deposit slips home with me because I was so conscience of people staring at me at the bank. I needed help filling it out. I'd sometimes ask the people at the bank to help—some did, some didn't. I practiced writing numbers over and over again. I am much better at it now. I can write up to 12,000...I need help after that! I have my own little way of figuring things out.

Preschool

Working at the preschool was not very glamourous—I mostly changed diapers, cleaned classrooms—the dirtier jobs—and I did every one of them! I also had to cook, which I was very good at, and make snacks for the kids. I had to remember everything they told me because I couldn't read or jot down notes. I worked there for a year and a half. I was happy to get the pay and loved working with the children. It wasn't a lot, but I remember when I worked from morning to midnight without *any* pay.

It was here that I met my first friends. People had a hard time understanding me but it was my boss, Liz, and two other women I worked with, Vickie and Annette, that I felt drawn to right away. The short time we worked together—I worked there the longest out of us three—cemented our friendships and we still get together from time to time, up until this day. I was assigned as a teacher's assistant or 'TA' to work with Annette.

Annette

Annette and I seemed to connect right away. She understood my broken English pretty well, even over the phone. We both had a way of raising our voices when we became emotional. At times, it sounded as if we were screaming back and forth at each other. She was more laid back than I was—I was so used to working, working, working so I wouldn't get yelled at, so it was hard for me at first to slow down, and be social as I did my work. I would complete a task and then hurry to get the next one done. Annette would say, "Slow down, Shari, relax. It'll get done. You don't have to work yourself to death." I had been so isolated for so long, even in the middle of people all around me, that I didn't yet have the social skills of interacting with others on the job. I was always in the background, invisible, and now I had to learn how to be just a regular person, working a job. It hadn't dawned on me this was an issue until I started working with Annette.

I got along so well with Annette and she had lived so close to the preschool like I now did, that she'd often ask me if I wanted to take a walk with her. She didn't have her driver's license then and of course I didn't drive, so walking was a part of life for us both.

One day after work we went on a long walk. It was then I got up the nerve to tell her my story. "Annette," I said, "I tell you something, okay?" We kept up a good pace as we strode down the sidewalk away from the preschool. I saw her wave at another coworker who had just pulled out of the parking lot and drove past us on the street. "Good for you guys! Walk off those pounds." The driver joked as Annette shouted back and then turned her attention back to me. "Go ahead..." she replied. "Okay,...I tell you my story." I took a deep breath and continued. "I was slave in Taiwan to Old Lady. I sold to her when I only seven. Came to U.S. and run away from her." Annette was oddly quiet while my incredible story came spilling out of me, in short choppy words; me, repeating most of the phrases I knew over and over again, hoping to convey a deeper meaning with the few words I did know. So often human trafficking involves prostitution, abuse and even rape so I think Annette wasn't sure if she should ask me details about what happened, in case these horrible things occurred. But she listened intently and I felt her concern for me in the silence.

I can't tell you how good it felt to tell her the truth about myself! I had to know if she would feel the same about me after I told her, that she would still want to be my friend. Now the wondering was over and she was still there with me. I don't remember how she reacted exactly, I do know when I got to the part about how I escaped she blurted out, "Oh my gosh! That is SO crazy!"

Most people don't really know what to say when they find out what happened to me. A few react with, "Wow! I can't believe this happened to you!" or "Oh, my goodness," or even, "I'm so sorry this happened." I understand how incredible this may seem. You can't always tell from the outside what someone has gone through on the inside.

Revealing my past to Annette gave me the strength to tell my boss, Liz, my story, too, who in turn told Vickie, and now those in my closest circle at work knew my story and they all made a huge effort, wanting to help me whenever they could.

Vickie

Vickie often took me shopping. We'd go to the grocery store and we'd walk up and down the aisles. Vickie didn't rush me. She wanted me to enjoy the task and make decisions. She'd help me read different signs and stuff and then when we got to the checkout, she'd help me to pay. I was able to open a checking account with the help of my caseworker, but writing checks was still hard for me to do. Vickie tried to teach me. "You put the date here and then write the amount there," she pointed with her finger, "then you have to spell out the amount on this line as well." Most of the time she'd end up writing the amount in and I would just sign my name below. She'd even go with me to the bank sometimes when I needed help.

I remember going make-up shopping with her. Both Vickie and Annette would tease me about my 'expensive tastes.' Living with The Old Lady and her Daughter who were so particular about what they wore and how they looked and then living with Judy and her extravagant lifestyle, made me desire finer things, especially when I lived so deprived of the most basic of needs for so long.

"Hey, wanna go to Walgreens on Saturday?" Vickie asked one day. "They have a big selection of make-up and the prices are pretty cheap." "Vickie—you so good with money, listen to husband all time…you more Asian than me!" I replied with a smile. She laughed and we made the date. Saturday came and Vickie pulled up to the house. "Ready?" she called to me as I came out. I couldn't wait.

"What about this color?" Vickie suggested, pulling out a few different shades of eye shadow from the display on the wall. "Oooo..." I said, as I reached my hand out towards the green one. "I love, love, love green one!" I said, almost giggling. This was so much fun! I was shopping for make-up with my friend. We must have spent hours going through all the eye shadow, lipstick, and nail polish. There were so many pretty colors "Hey Shari, I want you to have this one. My treat." Vickie offered. She put the pretty green eyeshadow I had 'oooed' at earlier in the basket, then headed to the register and set the items on the counter. The lady rung them up and put them in a bag. "Thank you for shopping Walgreens," the clerk said as we turned to walk out. I put my hand on Vickie's shoulder and she turned to look at me. "Thank you. Thank you so much." I said, looking in her eyes with meaning. Yes, of course I was thankful for the make-up, but what I really wanted to say was, "Thank you for being my friend. Thank you for 'girl time,' being silly, being so 'normal' like girlfriends do; it means a lot to me."

Money, Shopping and Me

I really didn't know how to budget, so money went fast. There were so many new things I needed to learn and I just had to figure it all out on my own.

I only worked with really little kids, so I didn't learn much from them; co-workers would often point out, "You don't know how to spell that?" and they would help me. Spelling was hard for me. They would help me write. I had to fill out paperwork for my job; not everyone knew my story, but everyone was very helpful towards me.

Life on My Own

One day I was in a hurry and Annette asked me why. "I have to go, walk dog." I usually walked home from time to time to walk Elsa's dog on lunch break. Annette looked me in the eyes and said, "You know, you are free now, you don't have to do that." I guess I'd felt like I had to, after all, Elsa let me stay there. We talked about other things that I could do rather than live where I was now. I looked at her and it was like a light went on inside. "I remember when I got out on my own," Annette continued. "I lived with a bunch of roommates. It was kind of crowded, but it was a lot of fun—and pretty cheap. Why don't we look in the paper and see if we can find a room for you to rent, maybe close by, so you can still walk to work?" I remember thinking, "What a great friend! I am so thankful that God has given me such a good friend in Annette."

So I found a place to rent with roommates on 23rd street. The rent was $635 a month. It was for only a room with a shared living room, bathroom and kitchen with several other roommates. The guy renting it seemed nice, so I took it. This was my first place by myself. I didn't have a bed so I saved up for one. I was now truly on my own. When I told Elsa I was moving out, she seemed a little upset. I was so very tired. I was going through so much emotionally at the time. I was finding it very hard to sleep. I'd be afraid to go to bed at night, wondering if somehow I'd be sent back to that family, forced to live with them again. I never told Elsa about the dreams nor the stress I carried, pretending everything was okay. This made it difficult on our relationship. I think she did understand, she just wanted the best for me.

The Nightmares

I began having these dreams—nightmares really—where I would see that Old Lady's face, angry, and hear her calling me names, telling me, "No one wants you; no one will ever want you, you worthless girl! I gave you a place to stay when no one would and you treat me like this?! You thief and whore! I know who you really are inside...you are a slave...you will always be a slave!"

I'd wake up sweating and my heart would be pounding out of my chest. It only got worse and I was starting to have these same feelings during the day, too. I didn't know what was happening to me. Then on the one-year anniversary of my escape something frightening happened.

August 18, 2006

"Happy Birthday, Shari!" a coworker said one day. I had told everyone that although I didn't know my real birthday, the day I escaped my life of slavery would be my new birthday from now on. I had never celebrated a birthday in my life before, so I made a determined effort that this day would always be a big day to me. However, as special as I wanted today to be, I was struggling with anxiety and was feeling pretty bad. "Let's go out and celebrate! We'll get a cake and everything." My friends said. I smiled and said, "Yeah, yeah, thank you!" but I felt so strange inside. I was there but I wasn't there at the same time. We all met at a local restaurant and we ate and I got presents. The best part was when they all sang, "Happy Birthday!" and I blew out the candles on the cake. I forced myself to appear happy, which I was, but something was just not right.

As the evening wound down, I felt physically worse. When all but the last few friends left, I admitted to them that I felt so ill I needed to go to the hospital. "Are you okay? What's going on?" my closest friends asked. I told them all what had been happening to me lately—the nightmares, how my heart would race so fast I could barely breathe. I was having all of these symptoms now. I felt dizzy and I had broken out in a cold sweat. Then as I was explaining all this to them my hands suddenly went numb and my chest tightened in pain, and my face turn pale. I thought I was going to die! This is when my friends became extremely concerned. They rushed me to the hospital immediately.

The Diagnosis

"Can you breathe in deeply for me," the ER doctor asked. "How long have you had these symptoms?" He had a small light he flashed into my eyes and it made me feel sick as he did it. "Can I ask if you have been under any stress lately?" He wrapped a band around my arm and it quickly filled with air, pinching the skin on my arm tight. The anxiety was so overwhelming I had trouble answering the questions. I was finally able to tell him some of my story. "Oh...I see...well, your heart looks fine..." his voice trailed off. He had done other tests and after the nurse came in with the results, he studied them carefully and then he turned his attention back to me and concluded, "Your heart looks normal...no elevated levels that I can see...hum...I think these symptoms you are having are possibly panic attacks...or classic symptoms of what we call PTSD, or post-traumatic stress disorder. Usually, this occurs in people who have been through some pretty bad experiences for an extended period of time, like what you've just told me you have. You're not having a heart attack or anything. I can prescribe something for it, something that can help calm you down, but you're going to need to get some help dealing with all this." He began scribbling something on a pad of paper he had and tore it off and handed it to me. I couldn't read what was on it anyway, so I thought I would show it to my therapist the next day. He was a psychiatrist and had already given me some prescription Tylenol PM to help with my sleeplessness.

Therapy

Amy had arranged for me to see a therapist on a regular basis to help deal with the emotional trauma I had gone through. It was a struggle to find the right one and to feel comfortable sharing all of what I'd gone through. The therapist I had been seeing had an open session available that next day, so I told him what had happened at the birthday party and what medicine the ER doctor prescribed.

"Yeah, this should help calm you down. You should take this regularly." He said. "It does have some side effects, so you'll let me know if you experience any changes, will you?" He scribbled some notes down on a paper and he asked a few more questions before I left. The medicine did make me feel less stressed but other feelings began that at first I didn't realize were side effects. I felt heavy and less coordinated. I began struggling to remember things at work. But now deeper fears grew slowly stronger—I couldn't explain it, but I didn't like taking this drug so I stopped. I continued to take the Tylenol PM—without it I couldn't sleep.

Saying Goodbye

"Beep, Beep," the alarm screamed as I stepped through the security gate at the courthouse. Amy wanted me to go with her to meet someone there. "I think it's your belt, Miss," the guard said as he waved a large bat shaped wand over my waist. "We'll need you to remove it." This became so crazy because the belt was sown into my pants and I couldn't take it off! After quite some convincing, Amy managed to get us both through security and in time to make our appointment.

"Shari, this is Lucy, she is an awesome case manager who'll help you with whatever you still need." Amy introduced me to this young woman who was closer to my size and height. Amy was very tall and towered over us both. I felt sad but also a little angry inside that Amy was leaving. I didn't know this woman and she was going to be my new case manager. Why did Amy have to leave me when I still needed her?

Amy had done such wonderful work with the Task Force, but when the opportunity came for her to move to East Africa to be an Aftercare Fellow with the International Justice Mission in Kampala Uganda and then to process refugees for the U.S. refugee resettlement based out of Nairobi Kenya, she couldn't pass it up. Deep inside I knew she had to go and I was ready to let her go—I just didn't want to admit it.

Lucy

Lucy was very different from Amy. Where Amy was outgoing and vocal, Lucy was more reserved and quiet. But she was strong and a fighter and would be there for me no matter what, just like Amy had been. Lucy was also of Asian descent, so I felt an immediate connection to her right away.

In 2006, Lucy was working with the Victim Witness Program, a part of CSP, as a supervisor. She was new to the program but already had a heavy caseload—mostly domestic violence cases. She worked with the DA's office—everything from domestic violence to vehicular manslaughter. I was to be her first human trafficking survivor. With her experience and background this job would be both old and new to her. I had to admit I cried that day. I didn't know how I would ever trust

Lucy to be my case manager, but in time she would become very special to me.

Lucy was deeply serious about what she did. "I think, with a trafficking survivor, one of the most important things we can do is to give them choices." She once said in an interview. She worked with me, helping me to create more options in my life. When she could, she would introduce me to others who could help as well. This is when I met another wonderful friend, Sister Marianna.

Sister Marianna

"I understand you would like to learn to read English?" she asked me in Chinese as we sat across from one another. Sister Marianna was a Catholic nun with the Sisters of St. Joseph. She had begun volunteering time with the HTTF after her training in New York. Her focus was on education and especially helping those who were victims of human trafficking. She had been a nun for over thirty years, born in Hong Kong and living in Canada when she felt the calling to serve God as a nun. Lucy knew I wanted to get a driver's license but reading English was still so difficult for me, so she paired me with Sister Marianna for tutoring. Since Sister Marianna spoke Mandarin, which I also spoke, it was a perfect match up.

"I'd like to record some of the lesson with you, Shari, if you don't mind. I can use them, perhaps, to teach others," Sister Marianna said. She was a logical and very practical woman. She rarely let emotion keep her from what she thought was best for me, and from the moment we met we developed a caring and trusting relationship. I was always on her mind when she'd receive donations, in case I had any needs that weren't being met. So many times when I needed help financially, her wonderful students raised the money I needed.

God

At first Sister Marianna and I didn't talk about God. She taught me about letters and the sounds they made. I even began to write a little. Our lessons would be on and off again because of both our schedules. One day I said, "I can't meet that day, I have to go to church." This opened a door and slowly we talked more and more about God.

I started sharing what I was praying about with Sister Marianna. "I think I want God to help me find my family someday," I told her. She would always smile at what I said, but she would also be very practical in her advice. "And how will you go about doing this?" she asked. She always challenged me. She never let me say something without asking my plan, making me think. She was always honest and straightforward. She never lied or let me get away with anything. I loved this.

I remember once after she had helped me with reading the DMV materials, she was supposed to take me home. "We stop at Target to buy card? It Mother's Day. I want to give lady who help me escape card." I asked.

There were so many cards to choose from and they all had such pretty pictures on them, but I had no idea what they said. "You have to read to me so I can know what it says," I asked. She read them all and then I chose the one that I really liked. It was pretty expensive, but perfect. Sister Marianna, being Chinese suggested, "Why not buy this pack of blank cards and copy the nice saying on to one of them?" There was a McDonalds inside the store. I bought the pack of cards and sat at a table. I looked at the card and after a minute or two I said, "How can I copy this? There is no line for me to keep words straight." Sister Marianna went and got a napkin and placed the edge in such a way I could use it as a ruler of sorts. It took me about twenty minutes to write it out but I did it. She was a good teacher!

Whenever I needed advice or help I would call Sister Marianna. She has remained a good friend and protector of mine. God had brought her to me at the right time.

Chapter 15

Derrick

A friend at work had asked me one day, "Do you have a boyfriend?" I shyly answered, "No," All those years as a slave I had never been allowed to make contact with anyone, let alone men. "I have a friend. We went to school together and I've known him a long time; we grew up together," she explained, "He is a nice guy." She took a picture of me with her phone. At that time I was skinny and my face had broken out with pimples. I was probably 100lbs at that time and wore no make-up. "There," she pushed SEND on her phone. "If he asks, can I give him your phone number?" She had said all this as if this was no big deal to her. I answered nervously and burst out with, "Okay, I don't care," hoping to end the awkward conversation. I thought to myself that this must be a joke; she is only kidding. Who could like me? I had always been told that no one would ever want me and if I ever did marry I would be caught in an endless cycle of marriages and divorces. "You are of no real use to anyone," The Old Lady's voice echoed in my mind. I shrugged off my co-worker's words and went back to work.

A week later I was surprised to get a call from 'Derrick.' It wasn't much of a call. My English was still quite limited and the only word that I recognized in the conversation was 'dinner' and I just repeated it back to him. On Friday Derrick came and picked me up. He was a big guy, strong and gentle. Sister Marianna would later call him, 'a big teddy bear.' Dark hair and light complected, he towered over me. Well, most people tower over me, but Derrick's build was not intimidating. He introduced himself. There was a kindness I saw in his eyes that drew me to him. I always look in a person's eyes when I meet them and in his I felt safe and unafraid.

Dinner and a Movie

I grabbed my purse and we headed out the door to his car. There was BJ's Bar and Restaurant not too far from where I lived at the time, so Derrick asked if it was okay to go there. My answer to most things was, "Okay, I don't care," so I repeated that to him. We found a place to park and walked towards the restaurant. The place was packed. It was a Friday night and people buzzed around like bees hoping to find a place to eat and forget about the work week. We waited about thirty minutes before I heard, "Derrick, party of two; Derrick?" We followed our server to a booth all the while I just smiled and nodded my head to whatever she said. There were TVs on every wall blaring baseball, basketball, hockey or whatever sport might be playing that night. It was odd, but all the sounds felt soothing me. "I am just an ordinary girl out on an ordinary date," I told myself. I was sitting across from a strange man yet somehow I felt comfortable with him. I don't think the waiter understood our date, I looked so very young with a nervous break out of pimples dotting my face. He kept coming over to check on us...or rather me. Derrick—this big tall white guy and me, a skinny teenage-looking Asian. You could count the words that were said between us. I wondered what Derrick was thinking. I couldn't read at all, so he had to read the menu to me and explain each item, pointing to the pictures from time to time. My friends were always correcting my English and they must've told Derrick that, because he was doing that, too. I didn't mind, in fact, I liked it!

For most people, a blind date can be filled with many awkward moments, but I didn't feel that way with Derrick. I could tell he liked me as much as I liked him. Most of our dinner was eaten in silence with a few attempts at small talk, me hacking away at English and Derrick responding with a, "Yeah, uh...like, you know, uh kinda, yeah, uh…good." After we had finished he asked, "You up for a movie? There is a theatre here and we could see if there is something we both like." I was happy that Derrick was interested enough in me to want to keep the evening going. We approached the ticket booth and he read all the movie choices out loud. "Hey, look!" He pointed towards to the marquee at one of the titles, "Crouching Tiger, Hidden Dragon is playing. Wanna do it? And what luck, it's in Chinese!"

I don't know if it was planned, but I could understand the movie perfectly. Later, I would find that Derrick was a huge fan of anything Kung Fu and especially Jet Li. Then we drove over to his friend's house and visited until nearly midnight. Well, Derrick visited while I mostly giggled and smiled, trying to look like I understood what was being said.

My First Real Boyfriend

It was pretty late when we got back to my place. I was nervous, but I liked him a lot. He walked me to the door but he didn't try to touch or to kiss me. He said, "Good night," and watched me go inside and close the door. I felt safe.

I was happy inside. I knew he was interested, but he took things pretty slow, not wanting to rush things, which made me trust him, really trust him. "What if he found out what has happened to you, Shari? Will he still want to be with you then?" My thoughts echoed what The Old Lady might say, "No one will want you! No one!" but I was too happy at this moment to think on such things. I went inside to the little room I had rented, closed the door and went to bed.

I continued to date Derrick and it became a steady thing—going out two to three times a week. This was a time of transition for me, becoming a real person with a job, a boyfriend, trying to sever the past and get the justice I deserved. I felt like a rubber band, being pulled and stretched, twisted and sometimes extended beyond what I thought I could take. It was exciting and petrifying all at the same time. I had decided to let Derrick in on my past. We had been together for a few months and I thought, maybe, the weight of my past would not be as heavy if he was there to help carry it with me. Expressing myself was difficult but I knew the word, 'slave,' and with the coaching of my case manager, I managed to explain things to Derrick. Whether he understood completely at that time or not, he seemed to take it well. He didn't ask many questions and although my words were limited, he was a man of few words himself. Confident that I could now talk freely and have a shoulder to cry on, our relationship continued—slowly, which I was so very thankful for—but steadily.

Fire and Ice

Derrick and I were so different. I was very quiet and shy when we first started going out, but as I began to see things in Derrick that bothered me, I got pretty feisty with him. He liked to drink and party and many of our dates ended at one of his friend's houses—everybody drinking—and me, sitting there, unable to communicate with anyone. I was beginning to hate these dates. "Take me home." I'd say after several hours. Derrick would drive me home and then return to the 'party' for more drinking. We were starting to get in arguments and they were pretty heated ones.

Once I threw a plate across the room. I wasn't trying to hit Derrick, I was just so frustrated and I couldn't say what I wanted to say. I was angry, so throwing something got that idea across. "Calm down," Derrick would say, "I don't know what else you want from me, Shari; this is just who I am." This relationship was a constant tug-of-war. We both wanted different things from each other and we were lousy at communicating it to each other.

Derrick never fought back. He never pushed back. It was a good thing. It was also a bad thing, too.

My 'Evil God Mother'

It was always me pushing, moving, trying to move things ahead, find a life for us, but it seemed Derrick was always on pause, slowing things down, keeping us stuck. He was a big soft teddy bear, and just as lifeless when I needed him the most. We were just two good people who were so very bad together. After a big fight, I did what I usually did: I called Sister Marianna. Most people, when they are hurting, reach out to a friend who brings comfort and warmth, who generously doles out plenty of, "Ahh…that's too bad…" or "Yeah, what a jerk!" Sister Marianna was not that friend. "Look, you know how Derrick is, you knew this when you got involved with him. Why cry when it won't change things?" Sister Marianna always told the truth, even when it hurt. But that was the very thing I needed from her. I didn't need to feel sorry for myself. Too many years I felt sad and helpless; I never wanted to feel that way again. "Let's talk about what you are going to do about this," she began. And talk we did. She would give me as much time as I needed, sometimes talking to both Derrick and me while we were in the middle of a fight. Talking us down off the ledge was her specialty, but it was not sweet talking. She'd often say, "I feel like an Evil God Mother to you two."

So many times Derrick and I were on the brink of breaking up and didn't. He was my first love and I so desperately wanted him to be everything to me, and he just couldn't. I was changing so much at the time—that stubborn opinionated girl was being reborn and at times she was just out-of-control. Facing my past put my emotions in high gear. I didn't know what would happen as I faced court. I was grateful I had people to there to help, yet it was an exhausting process, and seemingly never ending.

I don't thing Derrick really knew how to handle all this either. Our relationship was still new and just telling him about being a survivor was difficult to do.

I didn't realize then that this would be a long and painful relationship.

Disturbing Changes

"Ahhh…" I held my head in my hands because it just hurt so much. I had been screaming at Derrick, throwing things and feeling out of control. I couldn't understand what was happening to me. Sometimes I felt like I was flying into a rage for no reason at all; other times I would fall apart in tears and cry for hours. I was having more and more panic attacks, which had terrible physical symptoms as well. This frightened me. "Am I normal?" I asked my therapist during a session one afternoon. "Shari, this is all a part of your PTSD. What you are experiencing is normal. Many things can trigger it…a smell, a look, a dream…how someone treats you. It can be difficult, as hard as you try, to turn it off. As you begin to work through things, the symptoms can be managed. We can try some other medications that may help."

I didn't feel normal. I felt hopeless. I didn't want to take any medicine; they made me feel so much worse. It was hard to keep going every day. Anger and depression flipped back and forth like a switch. But mostly I started to feel like I didn't want to live anymore.

As I walked out of the session and into the sunlight, I was in a daze. I could not feel the warmth of the sun nor hear the traffic in the street—the sounds of people laughing, hurrying down the sidewalk. The world was silent, grey and tasteless. The pain of knowing this was how it was always going to be was overwhelming. What was the purpose of fighting anymore? Why resist any longer? I still felt like that little girl, looking out of the window, searching the faces of those passing by on the street for the familiar one that would take me away from my nightmare—my mom, my dad—who promised to come take me home, but instead, hearing The Old Lady constantly reminding me, "Your family sold you to *me*; they will not come to take you home. This is your home now." I saw the cars racing past. "Woosh, Zoom," I felt the stream of air from their movement blow hot air on to my face. "It can end so easily right here," my mind tempted. "Keep on walking, those cars won't have time to stop. You won't even feel it." I walked slowly and purposefully, edging ever closer to the busy drivers, who were focused on their journey home, to lives they looked forward to and rushed to meet. The gusts from the speed of the vehicles passing me pulled at the sleeves of my sweater. I kept walking mindlessly. Did anyone notice? Did anyone care? I saw no faces only blurs of light and color as I walked on, ever closer to the street. "Deet do dee detta leet," my cell phone called loudly and repeated endlessly, forcing me to wake up from this Zombie walk I had begun. I hadn't realized how deep in my thoughts I had been. I was standing in the street, inches away from a car that swerved around me and as I reached into my purse to find my phone. A loud blast from the driver's horn made my heart jump—nearly causing me to drop the phone. I quickly stepped back upon the curb. "Oh…ahh…I mean, hello?" I managed to say. It was my friend Liz, whom I hadn't heard from in a while. "Shari…I just had to call you; I couldn't wait!"

Thank God for her call! What news she had I don't remember, but the good news was it saved my life. I cannot say enough times how God was there in the very worst of times to rescue me.

Transportation

"I don't know how ride," I said. "You teach me?" I asked my friend.

My first bicycle was a Hello Kitty bike. My case manager thought it would help me to get around long distances. This bike was a big expense, it cost $400. I got it from a shop near the beach. I can't tell you how many times I crashed on that thing! I didn't know how to stop at first. If I stopped, I fell. So

I kept on going. It was scary. All the cars would stop for me, honk and get mad when I would cross in the middle of the street. I would shout out to them, "I'm sorry! I cannot stop!"

It took two weeks for me to learn. A co-worker and I would go to the beach so I could practice riding the bike away from the busy traffic. She'd laughed at me when I fell and say, "Shari, if you don't fall you won't learn." I was so short my legs never touched the ground! After that first bike trip to the beach I learned how to stop. She taught me not to be afraid. I rode it to work nearly every day after that, which took just fifteen minutes now, and I rode it even when it rained.

Chapter 16

Facing the Past

"We'll need to get a deposition from you, Shari—your side of the story. It'll be recorded in front of the lawyers from both sides and 'The Family' will be there as well..." my lawyer's voice trailed off. *The Family will be there!* My thoughts screamed this so loudly I thought I had actually spoken it. I felt a sick pit in my stomach as I finally formed the words, my voice cracking as I blurted, "I can't...I..." I gathered strength. "I do NOT want to be in the same room with those...those people!" The whole tone in the room changed and filled with, "it's okay," and "don't worry, we'll be with you," but I couldn't shake the nausea and horrible fear that gripped me. I knew I had to do this but all the thoughts of seeing The Daughter again, staring at me, the memories of what she did, still so real and this new life of freedom so unreal, I had to shut my thoughts off or I knew I would want to run and hide. The true me inside was fighting too hard to let that happen.

"Shari, this is how we will show them that you are no longer a slave to them," my lawyer explained, "They have no power over you anymore; they will be there, doing the same as you, giving their side of the story. It will be a difficult thing to face, but you can—you will be able to do it."

She's Not There

The thought of having to face The Daughter and her husband stayed with me all that day. I knew The Old Lady would not be there at the deposition. I had a slight feeling of sadness as I remembered hearing that she had been so shaken when I escaped (and the fact she was over 90 years old), that she was put into a home. She didn't live long after that. I had only been free a year when I heard she had died in that convalescent home, alone. She had gradually gotten more unpredictable and paranoid in her last days and would often lash out at me for no reason, accusing me of ridiculous things, calling me 'two-faced,' and beating me with a cane saying, "I know you, you thief and lying thing, you listen to what I say and tell *her* everything!" speaking of her daughter. I knew her mind must be going and felt sorry for that, but her words hit me just as hard as her cane did. This 'grandma' had been nothing but cruel to me, always. She was dead now. It should be all over, but it wasn't. No, she wouldn't be there physically, but I still saw her angry face in my dreams.

Court Deposition

This was the first time I had seen The Daughter since I had escaped that August night when Judy sped us away in the night. I couldn't sleep the night before. I kept seeing their faces and hearing the horrible things they had said to me, "You're a worthless whore! No one wanted you, no one will ever want you; you stupid girl!"

I had been prescribed some anxiety pills by a doctor I had been seeing, so I took a half a tablet like he had told me. It helped a little, yet I still tossed and turned all night and felt exhausted. By the next morning, however, I was still so overwhelmed with the thought of all that had happened to me and facing my captors that I took a whole pill after breakfast and waited for Lucy to pick me up. The deposition was scheduled for around 10 a.m. and the drive was not very far. I thought I would wait outside the house, hoping the fresh cool air and morning sun might give me a bit of relief and a measure of peace. How could I face that woman again? I just wanted my thoughts to be miles away from the hell I endured all those years. Up until now, I could never tell them, 'no,' or speak freely without the fear of some terrible consequences—whether physical or verbal—to be unleashed on me. I had started a new life and did not want to see them reaching their hands back into it. They had always won in the past, would they win again? Would the truth ever justify me?

"Hey, I'm not late am I?" Lucy called out as she approached me. I was so lost in my thoughts I hadn't seen her car pull up to the curb. "You okay?" she asked, looking at me, concerningly. My hair was pulled back in a ponytail and I was wearing a long black sleeved shirt. I think I must've looked like my best friend had died as I wore the most serious look on my face. "I'm okay," I lied, but I knew she didn't believe me. "You can do this, Shari. You are strong—stronger than they are. You have made it so far. You won't be alone in this. We are all with you." Her encouraging words held me together as I got in the car. It seemed just moments and we were there.

The boardroom we met in was filled with people. Lawyers, interpreters, recorders—I purposefully set my gaze away from The Old Lady's Daughter who was sitting across the table towards my left. She sat next to her husband. I swear all I could hear was my head pounding like it was going to explode at any moment. I swallowed in a deep breath as we began. "Let's all state our names before we begin…"

I repeated my name, but I really didn't hear what I was saying. My deadpan face was turned to the side, fixed in an emotionless gaze. "Yes, that is my name," the high-pitched voice of The Old Lady's Daughter responded as she took her turn at introductions. My stomach was tied in knots as I heard that voice—the sound I hadn't heard in a long time. I had but a moment to think about that before the questions started. Question after question bombarded me. They were the same questions asked over and over again, and no matter how I answered them, they weren't acceptable because the lawyer would just ask them again.

I refused to look in the direction of The Daughter. I would not acknowledge her; I must stay strong and not allow her to enter my eyes, to gain power over me again; I refused to be afraid.

I felt with every question my weaknesses were forced to be shown. "Have you ever seen a doctor? What medications are you on? Why were you taken to the hospital? How much money do you make an hour? If you didn't want to do that, why didn't you tell them no?" All the while The Daughter would hear each detail. My friends' names, where I live and work, my anxiety and what I must take to calm my thoughts down. I grew more and more angry with every question until I finally burst out in broken English, " I'm just trying to re-member everything you ask me…and every time I answer it the wrong way—I don't want—I want—if you ask me, I want true, everything true. I want to say everything true. Because there are so many questions I say, yes, no, no, okay? I'm sorry. Why you want to find my friends? They know my story, they know what's true. Find them then. Okay? I not trying to hide anything from you, I not lie, they know; we are fine, we are happy."

I didn't know if I was making any sense at all but the re-peating of the same questions, the constant, "What is their last name? Where do they live?" regarding my friends, felt like The Daughter was being given permission to harass them and ruin my new life. Then when they began to interrogate me about The Old Lady, who I had called Grandma, and asked, "Did you ever object to calling her 'Grandma,'" I burst out again. "DON'T!…please, don't. This…she is NOT my grandma! Can you call her, 'lady,' or…you say always—because you al-ways say 'grandma'. Can you change that? Just call her 'lady' or call her by her name. She NOT my grandma." The frustration on my face made me feel flushed. I looked back and forth, trying hard not to set my eyes on *her*. I was so very angry. I felt attacked. But it made the fighter in me come out. No one spoke out for me, so I would have to now.

Breaking Free

When I look back at this moment, I see how important that was. The Old Lady was NOT my grandmother. She was NOT someone who could or should ever have held that title with me. She was never pleased with me and she never loved me. I didn't know it then, but I was surgically removing that woman from my heart.

"Tell us, ah, how did you come to the U.S...what happened?" I told them everything, I held nothing back, The Daughter just sat there, looking like she had no idea what I was talking about, trying to look so innocent. I was a volcano inside as I got to the part where I got so sick when my legs were infected, my words came sharp and forceful.

"This was very hard time for me. My legs...so painful... swollen...nothing would fit me. No wear shoes—no wear pants. Even neighbors, people...shocked at how swollen... told The Old Lady and her Daughter I should see doctor... they wouldn't take me. Two week passed before they took me to see doctor. Even he afraid to touch my legs. I see his face— didn't want to touch me, afraid of the sores...I could not believe I was treated like this!" Suddenly I looked directly at The Daughter, my face determined as I fired away at her with my words, "How could you treat me like this? You can still sit there—with that smirk on your face—knowing how painful this was for me!" I guess that was enough for the lawyers to hear as they asked we take a break and for me to take some time to cool down. Oh, how angry I was that they were getting away with treating me so terribly!

Pushed to the Edge

The break didn't change much as things continued as they were before with question after question. Sometimes my answers came with anger, sometimes tears, but the lawyers for The Daughter showed no concern or compassion. After my life was cut open there in front of them all, the question finally came, "You said earlier, something about, being suicidal. What did you mean by that?" I gathered my thoughts and gripped myself from the inside, for I felt the tears beginning to form and I hated for The Old Lady's Daughter to see them. "Because I was thinking of it a lot," I finally began, "I was thinking about many, many things. When I wanted to escape and when I escaped, I thought about things—all of the things that happened back then. That's it. Just many things I was thinking about in my mind. Of course, naturally, I would be thinking about suicide." The lawyer could not let that answer be enough and pursued it further, "You say 'naturally,' why do you say, 'naturally,' you would be thinking about suicide?" I could not control the tears as they begin to fill my eyes and I continued to let the pain flow out in that cold and uncaring boardroom. The Old Lady's Daughter sat there, unmoved, the lawyers, unbelieving and as cold as the room, rifled through their papers. My lawyer sat near me, but I felt no comfort or strength from anyone as I began again to explain. "I think about many things, because I was very sad. I thought about my grandmother—but she is not my grandmother. I thought about when I was little. I thought about how badly she treated me. She did not treat me like a family, she did not treat me like a granddaughter. Whatever I did she was always displeased. I will not forget. What I will never ever be able to forget is grandmother, judging me and my family, because we had nothing to eat, so she would accuse me of stealing food, stealing things to eat. This 'grandmother' would beat me—with whatever she could find near her—a bamboo rod, a hanger, her cane—she would hit me and say horrible things to me, cursing me, telling me I would have been nothing if she did not buy me."

The pain, the heart-wrenching emotion of being so unloved and uncared for forced the tears to flow—down my face, stinging my cheeks and chin. I pulled a tissue from a small plastic pack that sat on the large table in front of me. I wiped the salty streaks as the memories poured back into my mind. I was almost there again, with that Old Lady, with The Daughter, hearing and feeling the abuse. I waited for the translator to finish conveying my painful thoughts. "What I can never forget—what I will never be able to forget is one time The Old Lady accused me of stealing and drinking some of her ginseng tea. I was doing my chores, cleaning the kitchen when she went into a rage. 'I paid good money to your father, to your family and what? Now you steal from me! You disgusting thief!' I had not stolen anything from her; I would never steal…She grabbed my head and pulled it back, gripping my hair in her hands and pulling it hard. She refused to let me go. I struggled but I was so very small and she was very strong. She dragged me by my hair, down the hall towards the bathroom." Uncontrollably, my voice grew tight and tears streamed down my face, my lips tasting the bitter drops as I forced myself to reveal this abusive act. "She, this 'grandmother' of mine, pulled me onto the floor and snatching the filthy brush used to clean to the toilet, she stuffed it into my mouth. I was not a human being to her and never would be. I had wanted her to love me like a granddaughter, but she treated me worse than a dog on the street. Yes, my mother sold me, but even she would not treat me like this. I missed my Mama so much then." I knew the lawyer would not let me continue much longer but I had to let everyone know how horrible The Old Lady had been, how terribly they all had treated me and how they were now trying to turn my words, all this, into lies. I could not let this happen so I continued on, "I remember The Old Lady would only feed me food that was already spoiled and refused to let me sit at the table but forced me to eat in a corner like a mongrel. I thought a lot about trying to leave and find my mother, but how? I did not know where she was or how to find her. It was a constant flow of abuse—both physical with beatings and emotional with the harsh words and cursing. I never knew what I did wrong to deserve this."

I was done. I spoke out the unspeakable to The Daughter's face. I let the lawyers know. The truth was recorded on video, transcribed, undeniable. As I pulled more tissues out of the pack, the plastic crinkled loudly in the silent room. I wiped my eyes, lips and nose from the wetness of my tears.

The lawyer for The Old Lady's Daughter was unmoved. He even chuckled as he responded, "You've gone on a lot...I'm not sure it was even responsive to my question." My lawyer chimed in, "You asked her about her suicidal thoughts..." "I did," he replied, but he just had to put a dig in there not realizing his words stabbed at my already wounded heart. "...And I'm not sure the long narrative was responsive but..." I cut him off, as now my tears dried and anger rose up in me. "Well, that's my answer. Every time I thought about these things, it caused me a lot of pain," I fired back. He tried to soften his callousness and started again with, "I...," But I jumped in again. "No, I wanted to explain. I understand what you asked me. Why was I suicidal? This was the only thought I had, to terminate myself; take my own life. You do not know the experiences that I have gone through, if you had you would not be able to answer all these questions—it would be hard for you; maybe you would understand what I felt..."

Seed Sown

A few minutes of silence passed while the lawyer took a few breaths and then continued his questioning, without showing any acknowledgement to my tears or pain. "You only *thought* about suicide? Did you physically take any steps to kill yourself?" "I wanted to jump off a building—take sleeping pills but I didn't. Now there are people in my life that do care about me and I thought about them, but the memories of living with The Old Lady, trapped with her and her Daughter day after day—it haunts me still every day." I was mad as I said this, but it didn't stop the same questions again. "Did you *try* to kill yourself? Did you slit your wrists? Take too many pills? Jump off a building? Do any other stuff to actually try to go through with it?"

I am sure he was just trying to do his job, after all, he had to represent his client in court, but he spoke in such a sterile way, and almost mean at times. Did he wish me to reconsider suicide? A small voice egged me on, "Yeah…just thoughts, huh? I don't believe any of this. If it were true, why didn't you try?"

"Yes…okay? Once I really thought about suicide…I was walking. I saw a vehicle, and oncoming car in the street and so I stepped out into its path. I was still standing in the middle of the street when my cell phone suddenly rang. It was my friend, Liz. I snapped out of it and woke up as the vehicle swerved around me, honking as it went. Okay? Is this what you want? Okay?" More frustration and anger dried my tears as the lawyer once again ignored my words and went on to the next question.

They all wanted to paint a picture that I was not treated unfairly by The Old Lady or her Daughter. They claimed I was given gifts, expensive jewelry, and that my life would have been no different had I not been living with them. And when

I would explain my side it seemed to get me nowhere. My life no different?

"You shopped at Ross, right?" Of course I went shopping with The Old Lady, I was her servant, her slave. She leaned her heavy bodyweight on my shoulder as if I were her cane everywhere. I carried her bags, waited on her hand and foot. I never left her sight. I was not hanging out with her and shopping with my own money or there of my own choice. I *had* to be there. Did they buy clothes for me? Yes, once or twice a year but mostly I wore hand-me-downs given to me from the church. They had to keep up appearances. Buy me clothes? For three years I owned only 3 pairs of pants and one top. I hand washed my clothes each night so I would at least be clean. Yet the interrogation went on and on.

When the lawyer continued to harass me about an expensive present of jewelry—a so-called gold watch—I lost it once again and spoke to The Daughter to her face. "Gold watch? Why you make up such stories? Never, never ever. You sit there making up lies. You have always fixed things to make you look like you are in the right—but God sees; He alone knows everything that happened throughout the years as I do. I am so angry that even now you refuse to tell the truth. I took nothing with me that night that I escaped—nothing but the clothes on my back. I knew that anything that I had was really yours so I refused to take it. But one thing that was given to me—not by you or your mother—but a good woman from the church—a Bible that means so much to me. I could not read it then and cannot yet now, but I know that the words that God speaks are in that book and He is the reason I am here today; here, free from you and from The Old Lady that brought me so much harm and pain. It was He alone who watched over me, keeping me from hating. I only wanted to be loved and accepted into your family, but you would not have that. You lie here in front of us all, but He knows everything. God has seen it all." My anger had reached a point that I had to speak my mind to the lawyer as well, so when he tried to tell me I treated The Old Lady's Daughter to lunch, went shopping and other things of my own free will, I looked straight at him and said, "I worked for her—The Daughter—I had to go with The Old Lady. I did not do any of this because I wanted to. They calculated the time. If I came back late I would be grilled as to why. I couldn't speak English at all. Who could I talk to? Where could I go on foot that they couldn't find me? You hear my explanation and then say, "I didn't ask you about the time, I didn't ask you about this or that" then you strike my answer from the record and say I am not responsive! I can no longer calm down. You continue to ask me questions only to want me to answer the way you want me to! I can no longer calm down."

It wasn't too long after this that we had to end and reschedule for another time to speak but the damage had been done. I was angry and deeply emotional and the flood of memories that I daily kept back in the dark were set free to torment my mind. I was not okay after this. I felt completely hopeless and I wasn't sure what I was going to do. I had sat there answering questions for over seven hours and my energy was completely drained. I got up and left. Lucy was waiting outside the board-room to drive me back home.

I Lost, They Won

I was SO depressed after leaving the deposition. I had no close friends to talk to and although my case manager, Lucy, was so supportive and caring, I just couldn't express to her what was going on inside me. "You sure you're okay?" Lucy asked as she drove me back home. I sat in the car looking out the window at all the traffic and people passing by in the street. The truth was all that mattered to me. All of those years, all of things that happened to me; I spoke the truth, I faced that family—The Old Lady's Daughter—and I told the truth, but it didn't seem to make a difference. They always lied and they always seemed to win. "I okay," I managed to squeeze out of my completely exhausted body. My throat felt sore from trying to keep from crying. I wanted to just break down and bawl, but I felt it would do no good now.

I lost. They won. They will always win so what else was there?

"Are you *sure* you're okay? You'd tell me, right, if you weren't?" Lucy coaxed once more. "I mean, you gotta promise me if you're not ok you will tell me. Promise me—you gotta promise me, Shari, you'll call me if you're not okay." Still mind-lessly staring out the window I reassured her again, "Yeah... okay...I okay."

We arrived at my apartment after 8 p.m. As we said good-bye, I managed to stretch my lips into a half-hearted smile. "Thank you very much that you come today with me, Lucy. Thank you so much." I unbuckled my seatbelt and got out of the car. I didn't even turn around to see her drive away, I just turned and headed towards the door.

As I walked through the door I could hear my land-lord, who lived there with me and my other two roommates. He rented the house from someone and then sublet several rooms out, one of them to me. He didn't hear me come in, and I was glad that I could just go to my room. "Why is all this happening to me?" I cried out to God, my eyes too empty for tears, my heart so broken I could hardly get the words out. "I just told the truth. That is all I did, but still it doesn't seem to matter. They will continue to fight with me forever. How can they always win? I can't do this anymore." I saw the bottle of Tylenol PM that I had placed near my bed. How I just wanted to sleep, to forget this all, to be done with living this life.

I took the bottle. Then I went into the bathroom and filled a glass half way with water. I shook the bottle. Plenty of pills rattled against this sides of the container. I didn't hesitate but swallowed them all down with a mouthful or two of water. I mechanically opened a drawer and grabbed my razor. This was a bit harder for me to do but I angled the disposable razor as best as I could, pressing the metal blades against the soft skin of my wrist and jerking it quickly across as it stung and I began to bleed.

My cell phone was lying on the bed. I looked at it and for whatever reason, I called Lucy's office. "You've reached the voicemail of…" The message began and I waited for the beep and said, "Thank you, Lucy, for everything. You helped me so much. Thank you." I hung up the phone and sat on the bed. I don't remember anything after that, but I know I didn't care anymore. The lawyer's words rang in my ears as he kept asking over and over, "You only *thought* about it, didn't you? But did you DO anything? Take any pills? Slit your wrists? Jump off a building? Did you do any other stuff to *actually* try to go through with it?" I guess I hadn't. It was if the lawyer was calling me a liar, too! Well, it was the truth now.

Lucy had driven away, but I hadn't convinced her that I was really okay. She knew something was wrong. She was already late for another appointment and when she arrived, the time seemed to drag on. I had no idea how troubled she was over my frame of mind. "Mind if I step out for a moment?" she asked. She checked her office voicemail and heard my voice saying, "Thank you, Lucy, for everything…" There was something very wrong in those words. Lucy couldn't quite put her finger on it, but everything was not okay. She headed back towards my apartment, jumped out of the car and walked up to the door. "Well, her bike is here…" Lucy thought. "She must be here if her bike is here." After a few knocks, the landlord answered the door. "Shari? Yeah, if her bike is here, she's here. She must be in her room." He motioned for Lucy to come in and they walked towards my bedroom door. If she knocked at the door I never heard her. The door was locked. I didn't hear her when she walked around the back of the apartment to knock on my window, either.

An urgency rose up in Lucy she just couldn't explain. She left but drove around the block and came back to my place. "I know I was just here," she told the landlord, "but Shari's *got* to be here. I just called her boyfriend and he said she wouldn't go anywhere on foot, she'd take her bike. Can you get the key and open her bedroom door?" The landlord hesitated before he said, "I'm not supposed to do that..." Lucy is not too much bigger than I am, but she quickly cut him off in midsentence, "Either unlock that door or I'll kick it in with my foot!" She demanded. Without a word, the landlord got the key and handed it to Lucy. "God, help Shari to be okay..."

The door opened and Lucy saw me lying across the bed, unresponsive. She could see by my wrists what I had been up to and she called 911 as fast as she could. By this time it was about two in the morning and the paramedics arrived in the ambulance and transported me to the hospital. Lucy followed them in her car. Though I had no memory of it, Lucy stayed there in ER with me until the pills had been flushed from my system, I was bandaged and given a room. Derrick was out of town at the time, so Lucy called his mother who also came and waited at the hospital. When I woke up, I found myself in a hospital bed with my robe and slippers on a chair near me. I thanked God that Lucy was there to save my life. I will always be thankful that she came back to check on me. I thank God every day for my life.

My Family of Friends

Lucy was not the only one who cared for me. I am so blessed to have a family of such wonderful friends. Although I have little memory of my hospital stay, I know Annette showed up for a visit because she had to tell me what happened when she came in the room. "Shari, Liz and I heard you were in the hospital and had to come see you right away." Annette explained. My boss, Liz, who was such a wonderful friend saw I had been struggling. She even stayed over one evening when I was feeling pretty depressed. She slept on the floor, too concerned to leave one night. "If it's okay, let me stay over…I just want to make sure you're okay," she pleaded. The girls at work could see things were bad. I was crying all the time. I had just started counseling and during those sessions the past came up. The counselor would have me draw pictures of the abuse and this added to everything I was going through and I just couldn't handle it all at the time.

I really didn't want anyone coming over at that time, but Liz had insisted. I didn't want to live anymore so I think I scared the heck out of her.

"Liz and I were out having drinks the other night and we got a call—'Shari is in the hospital.' I had to come to see how you were." Annette continued on. "You were just lying there, Shari, in the bed. You were so still, with bandages around your wrists. And then I saw you had this bandana on your head…you know, wrapped around your forehead. The word 'NUTS' was written on it. I gasped and was thinking like, 'Oh, no! They think you're crazy!' I didn't realize it was an allergy alert—that you were allergic to nuts!" I burst out laughing. Annette laughed, too. I laughed so hard, tears rolled down my face. How could I ever feel like life is not worth living? I again remember my mother's words, "Today might be a bad day, but it will be better tomorrow." I would be in the hospital for a few more days and would find out not long after this that my struggle with this family was finally over! There were still many bad days to come, but I would remain thankful that my past was steadily being put behind me for good, and for that, I will forever be thankful.

Derrick and I

It wasn't long after this that Derrick and I moved in together. It was sometime in 2008. He still had trouble knowing how to help me through my past, but he loved me and was willing to work on things. We still fought a lot but I loved him, too, and wanted things to get better.

I was so relieved that I would not have to face that family who enslaved me ever again. There were times when I would be with friends driving about when I would see The Daughter. Once when Judy and I were driving to the mall, she pulled up to the light right next to us. I ducked down so she couldn't see me. My heart would race each time things like this would happen and I'd feel those awful feelings once again—and time didn't make everything magically go away.

Derrick and I later moved to a nicer apartment; I could see him struggle with his commitment to me, but I didn't know how to handle it.

I was still working with children, but my new job was farther away and Derrick would drive me there. He would be mad that I still hadn't gotten my driver's license yet, but I couldn't ride my bike, it was too far. He wasn't working then and spent more time partying and sleeping in late. I wanted to get more serious about us; he did not.

Moving Out

"We're just moving too fast. I feel like our fire kinda died out. I think we should break up," Derrick said when he had gotten home one night. I wasn't sure what he was trying to tell me. We had been living together for a while. "You know, I had, like—what's those attacks you get? Anxiety attacks? I was in the car thinking about us getting married and I just freaked out." I looked at him, shocked. He felt pressured by me to buy a ring and get engaged. Now I understood. He didn't want to be with me. The Old Lady's words came back to me, "Even if you did find a man—get married—he won't treat you right; he will never want to stay with you." I couldn't control my tears. I started crying and I couldn't stop. "Well, maybe we could fix it—don't cry, Babe—but we gotta slow down. You need to slow down and stop pressuring me." Our lease at this place was nearly up so the decision was made.

Derrick found a place of his own near the beach and I signed my own lease for a two bedroom. We lived apart but we'd stay over at each other's apartments while trying to slowly build things back up…but our relationship was never truly repaired after that break-up. Our fights didn't stop and they were still pretty heated. Our friends were scared, saying things like, "What the hell?! You guys fight like that?!" Totally loud fights…I worried about the neighbors. And our clashes always revolved around the same issues—Derrick wanted to go out and drink with his friends and I wanted him to stay home and be with me. I liked to shop and he didn't. I'd go out with my friends shopping; He'd go to Vegas with his friends. We were pretty equal in who started the fights. My friends would tell me this relationship just wasn't working. I didn't care. I desperately wanted him to love me in the way I needed, but he just couldn't.

Gizmo

I had wanted a dog for a long time. I had remembered how The Daughter's dog had been such a good friend to me. Once after we'd had an argument, Derrick came home with Gizmo. He had known how much I wanted a dog. He was so sweet that way. I loved my little Pekingese dog. He was so cute and he'd follow me everywhere. But now I had to move and my little Gizmo could not go with me. The apartment I moved to would not allow dogs. I was heart broken. Hannah had taken some pictures of him and sent them to her friends. " I am so sorry, Gizmo," I said with tears in my eyes, "I cannot keep you." I hugged him and cried and cried. I knew Derrick couldn't take him either. I loved him so much I had to find a place for him. "Good news, Shari," my friend said. "A lady I know has a Pekingese and wants Gizmo to come be a friend for her dog." I was still sad but there was nothing else I could do. I felt like I was going backwards at times. Here I was alone again in a two bedroom apartment. I had to talk things out with Derrick. I wanted so much to marry him and start a family of my own.

Section III

Chapter 17

Survivor's Groups

As much as there was a victim in me, there was a fighter inside me, too. Since I was a little girl I have always had an anger towards injustice. When my sister was taken away, given up for adoption, I was just seven years old, but I knew then I was a fighter and though many times I wouldn't fight for myself, that fighter was in there, waiting, growing stronger in spite of my circumstances.

Counseling is a big part of a survivor's recovery. Maybe that's what started the process of setting that fighter in me free. And just like anything or anyone that has been chained up for so long, when it's finally set free, it runs wild for a time. My feelings were like that—I could cry or burst out in anger at times, mostly at Derrick, but I needed a way to direct the passion I had, the intolerance I felt towards injustice. It was at this time I got involved in a wonderful project—running a Survivor's Group. A 'survivor' is a person who has been involved as a human trafficking victim, who is no longer a 'victim,' but one who has gained freedom and now must learn to support themselves (and the children they may have brought with them) out of that way of life. I had help to escape the family that held me captive and I thank God for the Task Force, but I had to learn to live on my own, to break that victim mentality, and live the dream that was still inside of me. This passion to truly live my life burned so furiously in my heart that I knew I had to use it to help others, to set their passions on fire, to challenge them to stop depending on others and 'the system' and do more than just 'survive.'

Amy Returns

In 2009, my first case manager Amy Henry, returned from Africa. She began working with The Salvation Army. I was so happy to see her again. Lucy was still my case manager, but I was doing well enough to graduate the Task Force program the following year, no longer requiring a case manager. Amy and I would get together from time to time just to visit and talk about life. That's when I told her how much I wanted to help others who had been in my situation.

Amy had been to a Survivor's Caucus, a community of survivors of human trafficking who gathered together to encourage peer-to-peer mentorship and survivor-led advocacy groups and she really saw a need for something like this that could be implemented with the HTTF. I was thrilled she thought of me to be a part of getting that started. "I see the passion in you, Shari. You have such a strong fighting spirit in you. Really, you're a feisty, stubborn girl—just what is needed to help other survivors become more independent, like you," Amy said with a smile. I knew what she was talking about. She had known me as the shy, scared victim when I first escaped, and as the stubbornly outspoken survivor that I was today.

"What if survivors could meet together to encourage one another, learn life skills, make connections?" Amy continued. "Many survivors, even though they have gone out on their own, still have many needs…hopefully, we can fill this gap and bring them together to build relationships and help them to face everyday challenges."

Eventually Mimi, a Task Force administrator, and Patricia, a Salvation Army administrator who volunteered with the Task Force, would be involved. "It should be survivor led, but we could have volunteer facilitators help with setting up some life skills workshops and inviting survivors willing to attend," Amy suggested. "Any outside help such as setting up a workshop on budgeting or whatever, staff can help with," Mimi chimed in. This idea was so exciting, I could hardly think of anything else. Maybe I couldn't stand up for myself all of those years I was a slave, but I can be a big voice now. "I want to do this; yes, I do this!" I told them.

The first group met at The Salvation Army Office. Patricia and I were there. Just a few attended. But slowly more and more survivors came. I wanted the focus to be on fun things, connecting to each other and solving problems, not on being a victim—but on being a survivor.

Meetings would last two hours or more, keeping a casual format. People introduce themselves and are allowed to share, if they are comfortable talking, and we have snacks and drinks. Group leaders take turns leading so each meeting is handled a little differently. We address things like cooking, finances, parenthood or other life skills. I never miss a meeting and speak to each group, letting them know we are all here for each other. We talk about our needs. Do you need a job? Are your bills getting paid? How are your kids doing? Is your support group of friends growing?

Cooking Class

"Vickie, maybe you teach cooking for the Survivor's Group? Maybe bake something?" I asked my friend. She now had three kids of her own and she was so patient with them. "I think that would be fun! We could have a Christmas themed meeting." She said. "We can meet at my house." This is how most of our survivor meetings are—filled with encouragement, fun, and a friendly atmosphere.

It's mostly women who attend the groups, but we did have a man come once, for a while. Those who attend are from every nationality—English, Taiwanese, Mexican, Chinese, Romanian, Russian—human trafficking is a world-wide problem.

People who are survivors feel so lost. They get free and then realize they don't have any skills. How do they meet people, get jobs, feel connected? I am so proud of being involved in leading Survivor Groups.

My Own Child Care Business

I had a couple jobs working with preschoolers and really liked it. I was good at it and was able to take a few classes to learn more about child care. I decided this is what I wanted to do: open my own child care business.

There is a lot of paperwork involved with starting your own business. In order to get my child care license I had to read through the materials and write out my answers. I needed help. "We don't normally do this, but why don't you take the paperwork home to study? Bring it all back when you've completed it," the lady said. I was able to get a friend from church to read the materials to me and help me write my answers out. I knew how to take care of kids, it was just the reading and writing that got in the way. I had already done CPR and everything else. I was allowed to care for eight toddlers or four infants. I chose infants. It is still hard for me...billing clients and such. I work hard to stay on top of all this.

I remember some of those wonderful parents who took a chance on a new child care business like mine. My first three infants—Lilly, Big Bobby, Little Bobby, who were so sweet. They taught me so much! I remember Big Bobby cried and cried until he was able to trust me. I learned how to be patient with them and with myself; and most importantly, they taught me how to receive love.

The Interview

My life was becoming more independent. I still struggled in certain areas, but I was feeling more confident about what I wanted in my life. That is when an incredible opportunity came my way.

"CNN approached me, Shari, asking if any survivor was ready to give them an interview and I thought of you." Mimi said to me one day in 2011. "I know you had wanted to find your family—this might be the way to do it."

The Task Force was often asked by community members if any survivor might want to speak, so having CNN ask for one of us to be interviewed wasn't unusual. Mimi helped as a go-between—with the consulate, for interviews, knowing what questions would be asked. She did all this for me, too, after I agreed to do the television segment. As my former case manager, Lucy was interviewed, too, and walked me step by step through the process.

CNN had a special segment called, 'The CNN Freedom Project Ending Modern-Day Slavery,' where they highlighted the issue of human trafficking. It was hosted by Martin Savidge. Survivors of human trafficking from all over the world were interviewed and it would be broadcast worldwide.

Becoming Isabel

"Let's get some video of her riding her bike—since she can't drive. We'll add a voice over with info on her story." The CNN crew was here discussing how they would shoot the interview. I remembered the name 'Isabel' from a girl I'd had in child care and I'd liked that name, so I decided to use that instead of mine, hoping no one would find out who I really was. That became the title of the interview, "Isabel's Misery Touches a Nation." There were shots of me riding my bike—a newer one, (the Hello Kitty bike had long since been given to a neighbor's daughter); me reading a baby's storybook; inside and outside of my apartment and finally, answering Martin Savidge's questions.

"This is the mom who sold you? And you want to find her?" He asked. I responded with, "Yes,...yes..." "And what would you say to her if you were to find her?"

The camera was on me. This was my chance to let my heart be known. I had no more anger, no more hate for anyone. "If I find her..." I said, my voice raw with emotion, "If I find her I say, 'Mom, I love you so much. I just want to find you.'" I began to cry.

The CNN interview aired in the fall of 2011. Within three days, reporters began showing up outside my apartment. Amy was visiting me at this time, helping me to deal with all of this. After she had left, within minutes she was back. "There are two men who look like reporters wandering around the complex," she said. "I told them you weren't talking to the media at this time," she continued. Just then we heard knocking at the door and voices calling, "We just want to make sure Isabel is alright. Can we talk to her?" We peeked out of the window and saw reporters with cameras and microphones blocking the door. We didn't know what to do. "There is no way we can leave this place without them seeing us, Shari." And we didn't. We were trapped inside for four hours, figuring out what to do! This was so crazy!

Amy finally decided to call CSP, and they called the police. Several detectives showed up and helped us to leave—one of them remembered me, he was one of the detectives who had come to Judy's house after I had escaped that night.

This constant media craziness continued for the next few months.

From Case Manager to 'Handler'

Amy started working with me again after this because many media outlets were trying to locate me. One day Amy was out training officers in Lake Tahoe and she got this call, "Amy, get down here right away…we have the president of Taiwan calling us!" Things just got crazier after that. The Taiwan foreign minister was in the area and wanted to meet me. Amy became my 'handler', protecting me and becoming a go-between in all this excitement. The Police Department arranged for the Foreign Minister, Timothy Yang, and me to meet. Of course, Amy was there with me.

"I can help," Mr. Yang offered. The room was filled many other important people who wanted to help as well. I wasn't sure at this point if I was truly ready to find my family. I said I had wanted to, but I was scared. "When you're ready, we'll do whatever we can to reunite you with your family," he said assuredly. He was such a wonderful man. His help would prove so valuable to me. "Thank you so much," I said, as we shook hands and cameras flashed from every direction.

Chapter 18

Finding My Family

I didn't realize how the CNN report would generate such a tremendous response in Taiwan. As far as I knew, I had been the first Taiwanese person involved in human trafficking who had ended up in the United States. Even Taiwan President Ma Ying-Jeou was offering to help. As news spread to every news outlet in Taiwan, speculation about my story grew. Could I really be telling the truth? Was I just making all this up for the money? My family back in Taiwan found it hard to avoid exposure. I had no control over how this would affect me or them or especially the truth. The Taiwan media was going wild! I would be in the news there for over a year. Some of what was being said was not so kind.

"According to 'Isabel's' own description,...she did slave labor, was physically and verbally abused...another source considered this impossible...not to say 'Isabel' is trying to win

sympathy...but these doubts have surfaced...”
—Mary Chow,
Dept. of Communication Studies, PhD

It's difficult to explain how I felt to someone who has always been able to speak freely; for someone to understand the mindset of a person who was never valued as a human being, treated worse than a dog, whose motives were always under question and who was told constantly their heart is filled with evil desires.

I was told daily I was never good enough; no one wanted me and I was lucky to get even the little that I received. I was seven years old. Tell a seven-year-old child her parents sold her to a stranger and she cannot go home again. Tell her, although she is so very little and useless, she must prove she was worth the money spent on her. Never let her go to school or play with friends or play at all! Give her no toys or new clothes or gifts of any kind. Fill her head with condemning thoughts of hopelessness and despair. Make her serve you from before the sun rises to late into the night—every day of her life.

Tell me, how would that little girl turn out? Who would she become?

Many others were sympathetic to me. People on the street were interviewed, "When you watch this news, it makes you want to cry; it's very moving because it has been so many years," a young Taiwanese woman said. "They're still your blood relatives—you have to come back to meet your family members," a man commented.

News outlets dug up everything they could find, locating possible family members, even interviewing overseas Taiwanese residents who lived nearby, who eventually identified Isabel as 'Hsiao-feng.'

My Sister

"Shari, turn up the sound, look—you're on TV!" Amy and I were at my apartment sitting around talking while some Taiwanese TV station was on in the background. Suddenly, a young Taiwanese woman was being interviewed, holding a picture of a little girl saying, "I don't understand why our sister is not calling us." Tears filled her eyes. I looked at the TV in surprise. "Do you think this is really your sister?" Amy asked. I hadn't seen any of my sisters in so long, I wasn't sure. Was this my family? Could I trust them? "I just don't know," I answered. There were others we saw then—all over the Taiwan news, claiming I was their daughter, too. Amy really believed this was my sister. "Your names are so much alike...and she even looks like you!" she exclaimed.

Minister Yang had promised, if needed, to use DNA testing to make sure I found my true family. I was so excited, yet so nervous inside. The love I felt for my mother and family was real, but the truth was, they had sold me as a slave. Did *they* want to see me again? What would I say, how should I act? So many questions filled my head that my stomach began to ache. I was given a contact number but hadn't got up the courage to call them yet.

My Lunlun

Through the media the word came that this sister was mine and that my mom had been found, but was sick. She had cancer. How could this be? It took me so long to finally find her! This prompted me to make a decision: I had to go to Taiwan to see her.

I wanted to talk to my mom on the phone first. Still having some doubts, I wanted to be sure this really was her. I asked Amy to be there with me for support. I had no real furniture because of my childcare business, just toys, so we sat on the floor. I called the number Mr. Yang had given me.

The phone rang several times. There was a sixteen-hour difference in time, so it was the next morning in Taiwan. "Hello?" I said in Chinese. It was my sister who had answered. There were excited squeals as we reconnected after years of being apart. We briefly talked, but I was so anxious about my mom. After a minute or two she put her on the phone. "My Lunlun? Is that you?" I hadn't heard that name since I was so very little. My heart jumped and I gasped out loud. I knew right then it was my mother. I struggled to speak to her as I was beside myself with joy. My mom; I was here and I was free and I had found my mom! I had seen this day in my head over and over through the years and I was now living it. It didn't seem real. I wanted to be there with her and hug her and tell her how much I loved her. How I had forgiven her and now we could be a family again. "How are you?" she asked, "I missed you, too. You come soon?" She went back and forth between our native Paiwanese dialect and Mandarin, so it was hard to understand her. It wasn't a long conversation, but it was so powerful to me. I had found my mom!

"I did it, I finally did it!" I shouted when I hung up the phone. "I found my mom!"

MOFA Claims Isabel Calls Birth Mother

"Isabel, the Taiwanese woman who...worked as a domestic slave in the U.S., finally called her birth mother in Taiwan earlier this week expressing her wish to return to the country to visit her family in eastern Taitung. Isabel... sincerely worried of her 71 year-old mother's health condition, spoke in Mandarin, repeatedly telling her mother she really misses her, while her mother emotionally asked her daughter to come back home soon."
—*China Post*, December 2, 2011

The Ministry of Foreign Affairs and Timothy Yang sped up the passport process in order for me to return quickly to Taiwan. "This should take a few days, but don't worry, we'll get it done." I was told. And they did! Not only that, but it was arranged that all of my flights, hotels and whatever I needed were to be paid for. I was so thankful for this! Amy would come with me as well as Derrick. And my lawyer, at that time, rearranged his schedule to make sure he'd also come along. I had one more person I needed to come with me: Sister Marianna.

"Will you go back to Taiwan with me to find my family?" I had asked Sister Marianna so long ago. She knew I couldn't write in any language, so reading any of the signs or train schedules would be impossible for me. The Chinese language is the same written, but not when spoken. One word in Chinese can be pronounced so many different ways and there are over 100 different dialects. If it is written down, everyone can understand. "How can you find your mother then?" she asked. But I would not give up. "Go with me?" She looked at me with a smile on her face. "Definitely, but will you walk from person to person and ask, 'Are you my mother? Are YOU my mother?"

We just laughed about it, but I knew if I went, Sister Marianna would be there with me.

January 19, 2012

I arrived in Taiwan. When we left, a mob of reporters were at the airport, following me around, but in Taiwan…the media waiting for me was overwhelming. The Taiwan media bombarded us the entire time—it was so crazy! My little support group went with me everywhere, just to keep me from being trampled by them!

The Taiwan government hosted this trip so they came up with an itinerary. Amy made sure that I understood everything. It was unheard of for a survivor to be accompanied by a case manager to go to another country. Amy was such a good friend. The Taiwan government assigned a personal assistant and interpreter to keep us to our itinerary and help with travel. She was Paiwanese—a shy girl—with no experience with reporters. She was kind and thoughtful and stayed with us for two weeks.

Each morning she came to my room to tell me the schedule of where we were to go that day. I really hit it off with her the first time I talked with her. "Ms. Ho, we have a meeting today," she would say. She always made me feel comfortable. I trusted her.

Bodyguards were assigned to me. Going anywhere was so difficult. The bodyguards were even outside of my hotel room. If I went to the bathroom in a restaurant, they'd follow me and stand outside and wait. Even on New Year's Eve they never left my side. They had guns, too. A chair was set up in front of my hotel door, so they could make sure I was safe. They wore suits and glasses and were huge! "I feel so sorry—you have to stay always with me. I bring you some food." I said one night after they'd been standing, guarding me for hours. "You don't have to wear those clothes every day, you know, for me. Wear something comfortable." I smiled. I really liked those guys.

From Slave to Celebrity

It didn't take me long to get used to all the attention. I felt like a movie star! At first I was more serious. "Thank you," I repeated over and over in English. But soon it became kind of fun to be the center of attention. I smiled, laughed, joked when I was asked a question. "You are handling this really well." Amy told me one day. She spent the whole time dealing with the media, who continued to surround us so closely at times, she had to physically push people away. Amy took care of the logistics and spoke for me whenever she could. I was famous and everyone wanted to know what I had to say. It was scary and exciting, all at the same time.

We stayed in very nice hotels, free of charge. We went everywhere—but all I could think of was seeing my family.

Reunited

We did a lot of traveling, especially since my family lived in Dawu Township, near Taitung. So many memories came back to me—some good and some bad. Where my family lived was more country and remote so we flew into Taipei and then flew to a smaller airport. We were met by officials who drove us to where my family lived, which was quite a drive. Once a reporter asked Derrick some questions: "What do you do for a living?" He had the title 'engineer', so they were really impressed. So many of the questions they asked were about untrue rumors, we would ignore answering those ones.

The press was always there, wherever I was, recording my reactions to everything. I was nervous about meeting my family for the first time. How would I respond? I had been separated for so long, it was such a mix of emotions. The hardest part—which never crossed my mind—was the cultural difference. I was raised by a woman who was Chinese, claiming to be a Christian. She had customs and did things so very differently than my family, who were native Paiwan. There were things expected of me that I had no idea I was supposed to do; ways I was supposed to act but didn't. I had to learn how to be a sister again. I was trying to find my way back to my family and back to a culture I could not remember. Although they were my family, they were also strangers to me. Everyone had different memories about the past. We weren't sure about each other.

When I saw my family I was so happy! Of course, we started off with hugs. I hugged my sisters, told them how much I loved them and then saw family I never knew existed and those I barely remembered. "I love you all so much. You are my family. I am now with you again." When I said this, tears and hugs began all over again.

"Where is Mom?" I asked. My mother traveled back and forth from the mountain to my sister's home. She stayed with my 3rd sister more and more often because of her heath. She had remarried her first husband and both were in their 70s now.

I will never forget when I saw my mother again after all of those years. 'Lunlun,' her frail voice said to me. This was my mother!

I put my hands on her shoulders and patted them lovingly, then rested my head on her neck. I couldn't help smiling. My mom wore a bright yellow blouse and sweater, but I could see the redness in her eyes as if she were holding back tears. My sisters and family, my friends who came with me, surrounded us, but so did the media. Over 40 reporters watched as we stood in front of the door of my family's home, their cameras and microphones everywhere. I know the nation wanted to see this reunion, too—they had been touched by my story—but I wanted some quiet moments with my mom and family. After I felt they had enough photos I asked, "I just want to spend time with my family—have privacy. I know everyone is worried about me, but I just want a couple days with my family, okay?" I spoke in English. I hoped that they would understand and honor what I asked of them.

We celebrated by eating traditional food, better than what I had as a child when I lived with them. We talked and I introduced my friends and told them about my life in America. I was able to tell my mom some of what happened to me. I could see in her face how sorry she felt that I went through all this, although she didn't say a word. Later she would tell me, "I sent you away in hope of a better life."

My Father's Grave

"You were not allowed to stay the proper time when Dad was buried," my sisters said to me. "We must go and tend to his grave. Go with us, sister."

I was very tired by this time of the media hounding me so my sisters and I decided to go to our father's grave site earlier than planned. "Amy, Amy…" I whispered. "I go with my sisters, but I will be okay." It was just before sunrise and Amy was still in bed. "Where are you going?" she asked, half asleep. "I go to grave with my sisters. No worry. I am okay," I assured her. I had to leave quickly, for the media literally had camped out just waiting for me to go somewhere. I knew Amy would be there later and I hoped that as she left with everyone else, the press would follow them instead of us. We sped off and found a place to park and climbed up the hillside. I wasn't prepared for the emotions that spilled out of me. There were customs we did: the pouring of my father's favorite drink, the placing of items of food and such on his grave. As we each played our part in honoring our father, I suddenly began to cry. I sobbed and wept. I couldn't control myself. My sisters, each in turn, held me as I bawled and bawled. I don't think I cried this hard for my father's loss, but more for the loss of everything else. There were so many things my family had lost because of poverty and slavery. Things could have been so different; but they were not.

The Deal

The media showed up soon after we did and were completely obnoxious. They were shouting, pushing, shoving to get up the dusty hillside. Sister Mariana, Derrick and Amy had arrived at the same time. Sister Marianna tried to stand between my family and the reporters just as we began praying. "Could you just give them a little time...then they will pose for you," she asked. One reporter responded with, "No," so rudely. "Oh, want to pick a fight?" she thought and picked up a branch off the ground and waved it in such a way he couldn't get a clear picture of the family. When he looked threatening at her, she dropped the branch.

Amy took over from there saying, "If this happened to your family would you do this?" She was also now blocking the narrow path so they couldn't pass. Finally they replied "No." They were upset because my sisters and I had left early and ditched them. Then Amy offered them a deal: "If you let her have this time with her family, we promise to let you know what happens; we won't mislead you again," so they left us alone.

My 3rd Sister's Wedding

When I had told my family I would be coming to Taiwan, my 3rd sister thought this would be the perfect time to have her wedding. It would be a celebration, so family from everywhere, including everyone in the village, would be there. The media drooled at an event like this.

The wedding was to begin at 9:30 a.m., but by noon there was still no progress. By 3 p.m., tables were finally set up. I felt a lot of pressure on me. I didn't know what was expected of me, culturally, and I was buying gifts, jewelry, and spending so much money. I would look to Sister Marianna often for financial advice. "Set a limit on what you are going to spend and stick to it," she'd say.

The Rooster

My mom had a rooster chained up outside who crowed every morning. We joked that this was my mother's alarm clock. Later, as the reception began, we were all talking and laughing and I asked them, "What happened to the alarm clock this morning? He sleeping on the job?" Everyone looked at the plates of food we had in front of us. "You're eating him," they said.

We all dressed in traditional clothes for the wedding, even Derrick was given a traditional gown and hat. We looked great! I was given the chance to speak as well. It was a wonderful time with my family I will not forget.

The Letter

"What's this?" I asked, as my sister pulled a letter out of an envelope, smoothed down the edges and held it in front of me. "I can't read it, sister, tell me what it says." She looked at me and said, "That—Family—sent this to us." She read line by line the lies The Old Lady had written. It was a letter stating that 'Sharon' was in the U.S. and was healthy, and just wanted to let them all know she was okay." I was shocked. I had never known The Old Lady had been in contact with my family, knowing where they lived, and kept this from me. "We wrote the 'grandma' back, saying that we were glad our sister was doing well, but to let her know that our mom was not in good health." I blew up and began to shout. "How she not tell me this? She knew my mom was sick and did not tell me?!" How angry I was to hear all this. The stress of this news added to all of the other feelings I was experiencing at the time. My hands shook and it was hard to calm down. "How could she do this to me?!"

The Bike Ride

The scenery was so beautiful, we had all decided to go on a bike ride, thinking it would help to calm me down a bit. Sister Marianna didn't want to go. "I can't ride a bike very well," she said. "I only know how to go straight, not turn." I knew what that was like. "Come on, go with us…we'll have fun!" I told her. "Okay," she finally said. "I'll go and kill myself!" We had to cross a big street with lots of people. We just rode right across and never looked back. Poor Sister Marianna! Derrick peaked back several times to see if she was okay. "Derrick," she later told him, "You have a good heart. You were the only one who looked back to see if I was okay."

The Woman's Shelter

"While we're here, let me contact The Salvation Army. Maybe you could share some of your story with them?" Amy said. There was a local woman's shelter that housed women who had been abused and had nowhere to go. I knew I had to speak and encourage them. "Yes, I want to do this," I said. Amy arranged the meeting and we went. The women were from many countries, not just Taiwan. I remember looking in their eyes and understanding their pain. I loved these women and after speaking to them, letting them know how valuable and loved they were, I knew this was what I was supposed to do in my life. "I will come back one day," I promised, as I gave each one a hug.

Falling Apart

Several times during the trip I would have moments where the past would get hold of me. The worst one occurred when I wanted to stay closer to my family in the mountains. We needed a hotel but the one we found was a very unclean and run-down looking place. There were a few stairs…and white sheets…they looked dingy and used. And there was this smell…I can't describe it. It just didn't look clean. I felt like I didn't want my clothes to touch anything…or even to take my clothes off at all. Up until now I had tried to control most of my feelings.

As we walked in to the room, suddenly I fell apart. "No, no, no…I can't…I can't stay here…I have to get out…I can't stay here…" I screamed. I panicked. Memories from the past came flooding in. Derrick tried to help, but it just made it worse. He yelled and argued with everyone. "We have to move. We are not staying here!" No one wanted to be there, but he didn't know it. He thought I was being pressured to stay. That wasn't true. Were all the local hotels here this way? Nobody knew. I yelled, "Shut up! Shut up!" so he would just stop. Emotions were flying all over the place. It was just us four then—Sister Marianna, Amy, me and Derrick. We got through it. We found another hotel over an hour away and stayed there about two nights.

Extended Stay

I had decided to stay an extra week. My lawyer had to return to the states and Amy could only stay nine days of my three-week trip because she had to be back for work. Derrick left then as well. Sister Marianna had contacted a friend and had arranged for our trip to be longer. She had some connections in Taiwan and wanted to show me things, so if I ever returned and she couldn't be there with me, I'd be okay.

We stayed together and did all kinds of things. We were still mobbed, however, at every shop we tried to enter. Sister Marianna's friend was a famous cooking show host and her brother was involved in television. We went places with him and he entertained us. He took us to this night market. It was so much fun! I saw a jacket I liked very much. The girl at the shop recognized me and said, "If you take your picture with me, I'll give you a discount." Of course, I did!

More Bad Memories

"I have been to this market before," I said as Sister Marianna and I walked down the streets together. "The Old Lady took me here a lot. She would embarrass me so much by yelling at me…she'd yell, 'You never do anything right for me!'" I started to cry as I remembered this. Then we turned another corner and I saw a big sign that said, 'Freedom.' I wiped my tears and said, "Take a picture of me in front of the sign. I am free now."

Time to Leave

I had said goodbye to my family at the wedding, and all my friends, except for Sister Marianna, had gone back home. It was just us and now it was our turn to leave. I had promised my family I would come back as often as I could and call them all the time. We packed up luggage and headed to the airport.

When we arrived in Taiwan we stayed in VIP lounges to be away from the media. On our way back, we didn't have this access. The media swamped us! Sister Marianna didn't know what to do. It was just the two of us. She quickly called Amy to ask her to come to the airport when we landed. "You have got to come meet us—it is so crazy!" she begged Amy. Amy drove down to the airport, but ended up waiting and waiting in the car for us to get there. She saw many reporters who were gathered outside and managed to give them an interview, distracting them from us. I wasn't really supposed to talk to the press.

Life After Finding My Family

When I returned from Taiwan my life seemed so different. I had a family again! I couldn't wait to go back. I began Skyping my sisters and my mom all the time.

Sister Marianna had taught me how to use Skype. This had made things so much easier for me. She explained things and I could see it on Skype. We were able to get some textbooks this way. She held up the book she needed and we could find it on Amazon. Now this was coming in so handy! I had so much catching up to do with my family. I was continuing to get tutoring to read and write and had more of a passion than ever to tell my story, and to write my book!

Cindy, Beth, and Hannah

"Cindy, are you busy?" Jenna asked her friend as she saw her walking out of church one Sunday. "Lou and I would like to ask a favor of you. We're moving overseas and there is a special friend of ours we'd like you to…keep an eye on." Her eyes smiled as her husband, Lou joined her. "We know this precious child of God who has been through quite a lot in her life. We met her in the church's human trafficking ministry. God has now called us to another work overseas and we want to connect our dear little sister with some good, godly friends."

Three wonderful ladies came into my life that day—Cindy, Beth, and Hannah. They were all Taiwanese but came here to the states at different times in their lives, Cindy having lived in the U.S. the longest. They immediately welcomed me to join their home Bible study and wanted to find out more about me and how they could help. "Well, I can see reading is still an issue; let's help out with that," Cindy said. "I'll look into it and we'll schedule a day we can come over and do lessons with you." I attended the Bible study that Friday and shared my story with the group.

New Friends, New Lessons

"Why don't you get a phonics-based reading curriculum? I know a great one—Sam I Am." Diane told Cindy. "I used it with my kids." Cindy asked her coworker if she'd like to come with her to my house for that first lesson. The lessons would be weekly for a total of 50 weeks. For those first few lessons I had a house full—Cindy, her coworker Diane, Beth and Hannah. We met after work about 6 p.m.

The lessons continued for about a year. There were always at least two of the ladies there—they'd switch off each week, taking turns. When all 50 lessons were done, I was able to read the small book aloud without any mistakes.

Later, Cindy helped me to fill out a job application at Target. I was able to answer most of the questions on my own, but when it came to the section that asked about my education, I hadn't any. The manager was really nice about talking to me about it saying, "We don't just look at that…we look at other things, too." I didn't get the job. I didn't feel sorry for myself. There were better things ahead for me.

Public Speaking

After the CNN story broke I became well known. I was asked more and more to speak about human trafficking, especially at churches. My first-time speaking was with the help of The Salvation Army. I was so nervous! I couldn't write myself any notes then to help keep my speech on track, and when I did speak, I often wandered from story to story. I would only have so much time to speak, so this was a problem. Mimi helped me a lot with this, as well as Amy, and other friends.

I would usually start with, "I seven years old when my dad sold me into slavery…" I'd be amazed at the reaction it had on those who listened. I knew this is what God wanted me to do. Each time I did this I grew stronger and stronger. I would always make a point to tell them that I chose to be thankful, to be grateful for what God had done through it all; and to forgive, which was so hard to do at times when I felt so alone and abandoned, mistreated and unloved. I didn't know how I would ever forgive my family, or The Old Lady and her Daughter; but it was God who helped me to do this. He gave me those days of sitting in church where I could hear about His love, where The Old Lady could not pinch or kick or hit me. It was God who saw my needs when others donated clothes to me. And it was God who showed me kindness and brought Judy into my life to help me escape.

Meeting Sherry

It was one of my first times speaking publicly that I met Sherry Ward. A local church was looking for a survivor to speak at a special service highlighting human trafficking and I accepted. I practiced with Mimi, going over everything I wanted to say. After I spoke people came up to meet me. Sherry came up, too.

"Your story is unbelievable!" she said as she reached out her hand to shake mine. I didn't know then she had been praying about the types of books she felt God wanted her to take on with her newly formed publishing company, Square Tree Publishing. When she heard me speak, she felt God say, "Tell her story…her message matters." I had wanted to write my book for many years, but it was painful to bring up those memories and I needed someone I trusted enough to do it. Sister Marianna had tried to help, but I wasn't ready then. Sherry was patient to just be my friend for over a year before she asked me if I was interested in writing my story. "I am." I told her, "But I can't really write. I would need some help." I felt peace inside that she would be the one to help me get this done. "I think I know someone who could help with that," she said.

March, 2015—My Book Begins

"Hi Shari, remember me from the coffee shop?" Melodie asked on the phone. "I'd like to arrange a time I can come by and talk. I'd like to record our conversations; I can listen to your story and then transcribe what you said. This'll help me to write your book." Melodie and Sherry had been friends for many years. She now worked for Square Tree doing content editing but was willing to take on writing my book with me. And that's how it began. I would answer Melodie's questions, well—mostly I'd talk about whatever memories came to my mind while she listened. She'd interview many others in my life. This would continue for nearly three years.

I did a lot of crying during those times with Melodie. I still cry when I think of some of the things that happened to me. Melodie would stay for hours, recording everything. After just a few months I asked her, "My book done yet?" I had no idea how much work writing my story would be and how much time it would take.

Chapter 19

Finding Love

It was finally over. I called Derrick one more time. "Can you come get your stuff? I have boxes here that are yours." I told him on the phone. We hadn't been together for several months now. My heart was still broken and I loved him more than myself at times, but our relationship was never going to be what I wanted it to be. It had to be over for the last time and that meant everything of his had to be gone so there would be nothing left to connect us.

He showed up an hour later with that puppy-dog look on his face. "I still care about you, you know," he said softly. "I know." I said, without returning a "so do I…" Instead I said, "It not working…you know this…we move on in our lives… if I could change things…I cannot." I watched him load the boxes in his truck and drive away. Of course I cried, but he didn't see me cry.

Moving On

"I'm not sure I will make it," I told my friend on the phone. I had a Survivor's Meeting to attend and my ride had just canceled. "Have you heard of using a ride-share? I'll call and they'll send someone to pick you up." She said, "I'll set up an account, just log in the next time you need a ride." I went out front to wait for the car.

"Are you Shari? Did you call for a ride?" the handsome man asked with a slight accent, but it was hard to tell where he was from. There was something so different about him, he made me laugh. I made a point to remember him. His name was Omar.

One Saturday I wanted to go to the mall. I decided to take another ride-share again but when I tried to log in, I couldn't. I remembered that I had kept the driver's phone number who had picked me up before in one of my purses. I called but found out he was on a call and wouldn't be available for two hours. I decided to wait for him. It was funny, but he couldn't remember my address and ended up parking in front of the wrong apartment. This guy was so nice to me, but I really wasn't looking for anyone to date just yet. Months later I called him again to go to the mall. I felt safe using the same person for another ride. He dropped me off. Later he called. "Did you get a ride back from the mall? I can come get you if you need a ride," he said. It was then he got the nerve to ask me out for coffee. I said yes. It was fun to go out with Omar. I didn't feel any stress about where this would go, we just enjoyed each other's company. We had started to go out regularly. That's when Derrick called. "I'm pretty sure that you have my iPad somewhere. Can you bring it by?" I thought I had gotten rid of everything of his. I didn't want to go see him, but I did. I called Omar to drive me there. I wanted to know how I would feel if I saw him again. I felt sad. He looked miserable. It broke my heart. I looked at him—he was back living with his parents; he had no job. He looked at me. If I was with him, I'd be back in the same situation. I knew he wanted to get back together but I was dating someone now. I might've gone back with him if I hadn't been dating Omar.

I could see Derrick missed me. He cried. But I couldn't go back. I knew I couldn't.

"You have to move on, Derrick, find someone to make you happy."

More Speaking Requests

I have spoken many times now about my story, usually at churches or The Salvation Army. I believe God has led me to do this. Amy or another case manager always came with me. Once I spoke to over 200 people. I was scared at such a big crowd but it went really well. I was getting paid more for doing this—sometimes in gift cards, sometimes in cash. I'd usually talk for about 15-20 minutes each time. March is the busiest time for me. Much of my message is about forgiveness; as much as it is about my past.

I attend a local church. In one of the small groups I go to I met a nice Chinese couple who are pastors. They've encouraged me to bring the message of survivors to the church. It was hard and confusing for me at the beginning, to go to church, because of the family that held me captive, claiming to be Christians, attending church. I was so angry at so much in my past and would vent at God. But I wasn't happy doing that. In fact, I was miserable.

I couldn't read the Bible, so I used Google translate. I was led by these questions: Do I feel good? Do I feel peace? I didn't know what to do when I opened the Bible. Learning is hard for me. I learned to clean and cook really fast, but the reading and writing takes me time. It is still difficult to understand even with Google translate because of verb tenses and such. I understand the more American English way of speaking. I have forgiven God for all that has happened to me. That doesn't mean I don't get mad—I still struggle at times towards those who hurt me. God had His hand in all of this. How else would I come to America? I can't stay in the past, but here my story can be told. How can I tell others to forgive if I don't forgive?

So I work on this. When I speak to others, when people read my story, will they be able to trust what I say? I have to believe God will make a way.

Becoming Balanced

Omar and I continued to date. He showed me kindness and patience. I knew I loved him, and he loved me. My friends liked his soft-spoken way. He was rarely mad and put up with me when I was. But I had been slowly changing, becoming more balanced. He knew my past and supported my choices. We were a good match. I felt we belonged together.

My Wedding

There is something called a *time capsule* where a person or a group of people place different items in a box that tell a little about the times they grew up in, like some pictures or keepsakes. Then they bury the box, hoping in a hundred years or so the box will be dug up and all the treasures of what it was like back then will be gazed upon once more. Hoping time will stand still, the things in the box remain just like they did the day they were put under the ground or walled up in bricks or cement.

In January of 2015, the oldest American time capsule was found in the Massachusetts State House in Boston. It had been buried on July 4, 1795, over 220 years ago. The box was examined under X-ray to see what was inside and then it was carefully opened.[1]

One by one, each piece was taken out of the box. Those watching whispered a few hushed 'ahhs' as they caught a first glimpse of some of the precious old items—

Newspapers, coins, a silver inscribed plate by the famous American, Paul Revere—all had been buried and nearly

---

1   Catherine E. Shoichet, CNN January 7, 2015

forgotten. The time capsule sat there patiently, untouched, waiting for the moment it would be found and the items seen once again.

The day Omar and I decided to get married, I had no idea a time capsule was waiting for me.

Mary Lou, a beautiful young lady, was about to live out the hope and dream most young girls look forward to—marrying the love of her life and living happily ever after. Fast forward to the 21st century to that same city where Paul Revere buried his capsule, another famous Bostonian, a renown dress maker, was carefully hand stitching together the delicate lace of a custom designed wedding dress. The dress was beautiful and one-of-a-kind. Its elegant neckline dipped just enough to reveal the tiny pearl sequin clusters that, like little bouquets of flowers, splashed across the front of the dress, down to the waist, and continuing along its delicate short sleeves, all the way down to the hem of its simple, but timeless design. It was beautiful! It took many months to design and sew, but when it was finished, Mary Lou's petite 5'2 frame would fill out this masterpiece perfectly. A perfect dress for a perfect wedding. Why wouldn't it be? But as expensive and amazing as this dress was, it wouldn't be worn, as the wedding was called off.

Carefully wrapped in tissue and plastic and locked away in a trunk, a time capsule of its own, the dress was hidden to keep Mary Lou's painful memories from emerging. This silk and lace work of art, patiently waiting to be dug up and revealed once again.

The Project

I had no idea I would be the one to open this time capsule. My Bible study friends, Cindy, Beth and Hannah, were looking for a project. They would often pray and seek God in some practical way they could help someone and then that would be their 'big project' for the year. My wedding would be this project the group had been looking for, and Mary Lou would find herself in the middle of it. "A wedding dress?" she said when the group had met to discuss what they were planning. "I just happened to have a wedding dress," she said.

This perfect dress was put away, kept just as it was the day it was made, set aside, for me. I remember when I worked at the preschool, little girls would want me to read them the story of Cinderella, a poor girl forced to scrub floors and was treated terribly by her wicked step-mother. Clothed in her ball gown and crystal glass slippers, she rose from the ashes and became a princess. Finally, at the end of the story, she married her Prince Charming with the help of her Fairy Godmother. I wish I could've read those stories to kids back then, but of course I couldn't read, but they told them to me, pointing to the pictures in the books as they 'read' them from memory.

I was that princess Cinderella! How could anyone have known a beautiful gown waited for me to wear as I married my 'Prince Charming'? God is so very good to me, even for all I had been through, He made sure I was treated like His special daughter. He had never forgotten who I truly was, even if I had forgotten.

Seeing Judy Again

"Mom, I love you so much! You have to come to my wedding!" I told Judy when I called her to tell her the good news. We had a falling out on the way to lunch one day. This was a year and a half ago. I was struggling with Derrick and was just so frustrated with what everyone thought of the relationship. Angrily, I got out of the car. We hadn't talked since. The wedding would be the first time I had seen her since that day.

"You'll look just like a China doll at your wedding," she said on the phone. "I'll be there, of course, I wouldn't miss it for the world!"

The Ceremony

"Today is the beginning of your new life…" The pastor began. As I heard these words I thought, "I have had so many new beginnings in my life." How thankful I was at that moment that God had given me so many new starts, so many new friends, so many opportunities to begin again. I felt a rush of love and of forgiveness wash over me. I forgave my mother and father again for what had happened in the past. I forgave those who saw what was happening to me all those years ago yet chose to stay silent; I forgave The Daughter for her ignorant hash words that were so untrue and I forgave that Old Lady—for I knew the truth of God and of His love and forgiveness and was truly free while she was the slave—a slave to hate and anger all of her life. This was the beginning of a new life!

Chapter 20

Still

Life is never simple.

Marriage didn't magically make the past disappear. I am never completely free from the thoughts that haunt me and the challenges I still face. There were many goals that I hadn't reached yet: returning to school, getting a driver's license and expanding my business. I think of my dreams and then I think of my past. There are times I feel overwhelmed, even angry at what I missed, going to school, having a family. Just because I still feel such pain from the past, does this mean I have to give up on my dreams? My goals? I have forgiven those who have hurt me because I know God still had His hand in all this. How else would I have come to America?

I know I can't stay in the past and that I must tell my story. How can I tell others to forgive if I don't? Will those reading my story be able to trust what I say? I have to believe that God will make a way. I have to focus on my life. Others depend on me to help them face tough times, so I pray, "God, how am I to get through this?"

Have I still anger and hatred towards my captors? I am angry that I missed the opportunity to go to school and to learn? Why didn't they send me to school? Why did they not treat me like a true person? Yes, I fight these feelings still, yet as time goes by, it gets more manageable. I am thankful, every day, for where I am now.

Chapter 21

Coming Home

I have gone back to Taiwan now several times to visit with my family. It has been such a joy to see my mom, stay up late into the night gossiping with my sisters, eating the wonderful food my brother-in-law cooks over the barbeque. The time always goes by too fast and I miss them all over again. They ask me the same thing when I am there, "Will you come back to live in Taiwan?" My answer is always the same, "America is my home now." And it's true. I love my home of Taiwan; I love my family and Paiwan culture, but I am an American—at least in practice. I have such different ways now of looking at life—I can't really explain it. I am independent, not bound by money or 'what I am supposed to do.' I am free and love making a way for myself here. I am blessed to have two homelands and two cultures: Taiwan and America.

Writing this book was quite a project. I haven't yet the skills to write my story, so most of it had to be told, spoken in English, to an American, who helped me get my thoughts on paper. After I became free and returned to Taiwan in 2012, I learned about my culture for the first time because it had been lost to me. So much history of the Paiwan people was withheld from me when I wasn't allowed to go to school. I knew a trip back to my homeland with my publisher and co-author had to happen. But what I didn't know was all of the things God had planned for us—for me—on this trip.

Go Fund Me

Many people might think that after traveling back to Taiwan regularly and writing this book means I have a lot of money. The truth is that I daily trust God to provide for my rent and to pay my bills. I do not own my own home or have a fancy car (or a car at all!), or any extravagant possessions. I rent a modest apartment in a state that has a very high cost of living. I have my own childcare business, but one less infant, and I might not be able to pay my rent that next month. My journey has been a rollercoaster—I am not 'rolling in the dough.' Planning this trip with 'the team' started with a fundraiser. I didn't have the money to even pay for my flight!

A GoFundMe Account was set up. We had good results, but not quite enough for the ticket home. The Square Tree Publishing Team set up virtual meetings over the computer to discuss options. "Let's divide expenses three ways, that way, at least everything but the flight will be taken care of and Shari won't have to pay for that at least," Sherry Ward had said. I was grateful for that and for my team…things were looking up and I had hope we'd actually be going on this trip.

Missing My Flight

"Where's Shari?" Melodie asked, as Cindy, our interpreter on this trip, and Square Tree's publisher, Sherry Ward, checked in their baggage. "Just got a text…she's still on her way…some kind of traffic problem…" Sherry replied, glancing on her phone. Time was short and we'd be boarding in just a few minutes. If she didn't get there soon, she wouldn't make it through TSA.

It was just one of those kind of mornings where nothing seemed to go right. We had all planned to meet up and carpool together but I wanted to come separately from the team so I could spend more time with my husband. Traffic is always an issue in overcrowded cities like mine, but a huge accident was something I hadn't counted on. "Omar, hurry, do something…" I panicked as he wove through the lanes trying to get around whatever was slowing us all down. "I can't believe this!" I repeated over and over again, texting Sherry with my progress. It was going to be a close call, but I was able to get to the airport just in time to make my flight.

"Sherry," I cried, speaking into my cell phone. "I am here but I can't get my ticket. The machine. I can't…" Tears formed in my eyes. The trip I had wanted for so long was unraveling before me. I couldn't operate the kiosk to print out my ticket and time was running out. I started crying, no one was helping me for they had no idea I still struggled reading English and Mandarin. "Calm down, Shari, it's gonna be okay," came her confident voice. "We'll get you on the flight." What happened over the several hours was crazy, yet miraculous. I missed the flight but was able to get another one, my publisher making sure I didn't have to pay a dime. Sherry and I hung out that night, in the airport, laughing, talking and knowing that God was still at work behind the scenes to make this trip work out.

Mixed Emotions

It was a long flight so I had time to think. This was not my first time coming back to Taiwan, but this was going to be the first time tracing my steps as a young girl, down the street I lived with The Old Lady, walking through the market place where she'd hit me and poke me as I carried her heavy bags. The first time I'd see Yan Ming Shan, the mountain spa The Old Lady and I journeyed to daily and the memories of what those trips would bring up. I had to do it, but I had mixed feelings in doing it. I was quiet, not my usual talkative self. I was thinking, processing it all.

Our Lodgings

Cindy had booked all of our air B&B's for the trip and taken care of all of our travel details. I was okay with whatever she arranged. I was stunned as I opened the door to one of the places she had rented. The layout of it was exactly like the one I lived in with The Old Lady! I was so quiet for the first day.

Then I finally told my team. "I remember this room," I said as I walk slowly down the hall. "The Old Lady had this back room—just like this one," I opened the door revealing a pair of bunk beds. "There were beds like these, too, in there, and some stuff being stored, by her son I think," I continued. "It's so weird…yeah, weird, looks the same…" my eyes grew wide as I remembered that place. "The Old Lady…she had those beds but she wouldn't let me sleep in them…I had to sleep on the floor. She had this room and beds…I was not allowed to sleep there." This was such a strange feeling. It was like seeing the past, walking through a movie, but I did not feel afraid. I did not feel the sadness like I had then. Sherry, Cindy, and Melodie were here. I am free now. I am writing my story and this memory could not hold me hostage again. "Seriously?" Sherry said. "Wow! No way!" I began to share many more memories, the color of the door, the flight of stairs up to the rooms, so many memories that flooded in but it was as if God Himself was here with me, with my friends, so I could face this with strength and healing.

Late Night Conversation and Joy

I found myself talking to Cindy late into the night about these memories and how I felt about this trip. A healing was happening deep inside me that was new. So often in the past the healing was painful, slow, and sometimes, explosive. This was different. Joy was forming over the wounds. I had no idea that this whole trip would be one healing after another.

At times my quietness would fade, and a bubbly joy began to take its place. "I want to cook you a traditional meal from my culture tonight," I announced one day. "I need to go to the street market to get what I need." I thought of what I wanted to make, chicken feet in a warming ginger broth was the first thing I thought of. "I'll go with you," Melodie blurted out quickly. We grabbed the keys and purses and headed out the door. We made our way down the stairs and out through the heavy metal door. As it slammed shut and we walked down the sidewalk, Melodie said to me, "Okay, I'm going with you, but on one condition: I get to carry all the bags." A smile broke out on my face. I knew God was doing another healing moment in me so I excitedly said, "Okay, Meldee, let's go!"

The street was filled with vendors and carts and sellers of all kinds. The smells were wonderful as we wove our way towards the meat vendors first. "Ohh…" I said, looking at a display of various cuts of chicken. I spoke to the woman in Chinese, "I am making soup and need some chicken cut up for me," She pulled a large half chicken and a cleaver and wacked off a meaty thigh and leg portion and chopped it up, bones and all, and packaged it up for me. I paid her and as she gave me the bag, Melodie quickly took it from me. "Oh, yeah…okay" I said, letting her carry it as we hurried on to the next vendor.

"I need vegetables." I murmured out loud. I was so excited, it seemed as if we flew through the streets. I pointed when I couldn't remember how to say something in Chinese and it was placed in another bag and added to Melodie's load. After many purchases I knew I needed a ginger wine. I looked in shop after shop but couldn't find it. I had been down this same market so long ago and I had trouble remembering just where that special shop was. I stopped and asked a man, who pointed towards the end of a street where less shoppers were walking around. The streets were so full of people I had to weave through, careful not to lose Melodie in the process. This was the most expensive item that I needed so I got just a small bottle and paid for it. It felt wonderful to pay for all of these things! I may have been a slave and bore the burden the last time I walked these streets but not now…I was preparing a feast and would both be the rich lady buying it and the gracious host eating it. How wonderful this adventure was! "Wow, these bags are heavy," I heard Melodie comment. She now had about six or more plastic grocery bags equally strung on each arm. "And you were how old when you carried all of these? How were you able to do it?!" She said in disbelief. "And that Old Lady just hung on your shoulder the whole time, too!" I heard every word but my excitement carried me above them as I still needed a few more items to make my meal complete. We passed shellfish, noodles, pork vendors, enormous flats of mushrooms, vegetables, ginger and spices, and finally a man making tofu, carefully scooping great bowls of the hot chunky white mixture out of huge steaming pots and pouring it into thin cloths, pressing and draining it.

"Okay, I am done," I finally said to Melodie, handing her the last bag. "Let's go back so I can cook it all up!"

I couldn't stop smiling. As we passed a vendor who was selling some chicken feet, tenderly cooked on skewers, I had to buy one. "I was never allowed to have this on those trips to the market with The Old Lady. You want some?" I asked. Melodie's face squished into a "yuck, no thanks," type of face and she shook her head. I laughed and collected my treat from the man and munched happily on my tasty snack as we walked back to the B&B. I felt a strength I'd hadn't felt before as we walked back and it felt good.

I loved to cook when it's for the people I love and to celebrate life. The B&B had everything I needed to prepare this feast for my friends. I pulled out all of my wonderful treasures I had bought on the street and began cutting, chopping, peeling and preparing the dinner. I had so much fun! It wasn't long before the place filled with the smells of my culture and we all sat around and said a prayer of thanks. "God, I thank you for my friends, for this food and for all you have done for me. I love my family and am so happy to be here to see them again. And God,…I want to see my mom before I leave. Please, God, help me to see my mom again. Thank you, God, so much. Thank you."

My One Desire

Before we had left on this trip I had told the team what was going on with my family and how I wanted to see my mom on this trip. "I want to see my mother. I asked God to make it happen." I told the ladies. We had all been praying for this, especially Melodie, who had talked with my mom on Skype over a year ago. It may be hard for readers to understand my culture and how birth order and family structure plays such a huge roll in how we interact with one another. I am the 2nd sister, but being gone so long away from the family, my 3rd sister had taken on the role to care for my mom and to be there, especially when she was diagnosed with cancer. I love my family—I love my sisters. I never want anything to come between us. I pray for us all to forgive and find a way to stay as a family should, no matter what we have all gone through.

The Visit

"I will take you to see her, but be prepared, you maybe not get the chance," my 4th sister told me. I had been praying to see my mom and I knew God would work it all out. When we came to the house my mother was sitting around the back in a chair, enjoying the weather. "Mama!" I shouted. I ran to see her, threw my arms around her and hugged her tight. "Thank you, God. I finally see my mom. I got all the wishes I wanted. Thank you so much, Jesus! Please, I ask that she would prosper and that You would take care of her."

Things were not yet perfect with my family, but things were changing for the good. After a short time I headed back with my 4th sister to her house and ate dinner. "I know we said we would all stay together on this trip," I told my team, "but I want to stay with my sister tonight; I need to be with her this night." Sherry, Cindy and Melodie agreed and my brother-in-law drove them back to the hotel.

I talked and shared my heart late into the night with my sister. We talked about anger and forgiveness. We talked about family and betrayal and healing and the events of the day. My sister told me, "When you came back to the family it changed everything. God did something in our family. Sister, after you talked to me about all of this, I think I can forgive. Does everything that happen have a reason?" she asked. I thought for a minute and then said, "It was not my choice to come to America, but now I am here. I know God loves us and is working things out for us always." We were both quiet for a moment. I know that what she had been through in her own life was terrible, for she had been sold, too. I looked at her with so much love in my heart for her and said, "We all have a different story but our pain is the same. I want to write this book to help others. To help our family. It was hard for me, too, to forgive our parents—God helped me to do this. We must inspire others, help others by sharing our story."

"Do you remember what Mama used to say?" I asked. It was so late now and we had both climbed into her big bed and pulled the blanket up close, up to our chins. I thought back to when I was little and shared a pillow with her so very long ago, the same pillow I had left behind when I was sold, so she would not be without one. I felt the warmth of love towards her like I did when we were so very small; me—her big sister, her protector, even though I was probably only six years old. "Remember?" I continued, thinking of that last meal I had with my family, the sweet chicken and the bitter herbs. "Tell me…" she asked sleepily, "What did Mama say?" I curled up closer to her resting my head on her shoulder. I rubbed my nose with the tip of the blanket and sighed satisfyingly. "Life is like this meal, Little Lunlun; it is both sweet and good, but bitter and hard. Your life will be like this, too. Always be patient; endure and overcome, because tomorrow will always be better. Beneath the bitter herb is tender meat, to make you strong. Do not stop at the first bite; keep eating. Tomorrow *will* be better."

As I drifted off to sleep I thought about those words. I thought about what God had done that day. I remembered something He said in the Bible, "In this world you will have trouble. But take heart! I have overcome the world." (John 16:33b)

God had done so much for me in spite of all the bitter herbs that I have tasted. Beneath my current struggles there is sweet meat and I will not stop until my family knows God's love, for I know tomorrow will be better!

Extended Acknowledgements

Shari Ho

There are so many who have helped me along the way, not only to be where I am today, but to see that my story was written. All of them have become good friends and some, I now call my family. Thank you so much!

Deb

Thank you for being with me through my case. You have always been faithful in helping all the survivors and for that I am truly grateful.

Amber

Thank you for coming along side me in the survivor's group. You believed in me and that I could become all that I set out to do. You helped me co-lead the survivor's group and I am most grateful that you helped me open up my day care business. I couldn't have started the day care without your help. Thank you for believing in me.

My Amazing Bible Study Group

Thank you ALL for being there for me when I gained my freedom. You all tutored me in English and taught me so

much. Thank you for all the support on my most special day—
my wedding day. You have given in big and small ways and I
will forever be grateful to all of you women of God.

Derrick

My first boyfriend. You taught me so much and even
though we did not have a happy ending together, I am glad I
knew you. I do not blame you for anything. It was a time when
we were both changing so much. Your kindness to me I will
always remember.

Shelley

You are like a big sister to me. Thank you for every big and
small way you helped me when I first got free.

Omar

I care about you very deeply. I pray our love can be strong
enough to overcome all of our challenges. I always want the
best for you.

Gizmo

My furry friend when I was free. It was so sad the day I
had to give you up, but I had no choice. You were my four-
legged best friend and I miss your face.

My Furry Friend

My only best furry friend who truly cared about me when I was a slave. You always loved me and made me happy in a tough time. Thank you for never chewing my shoes!

Taiwan Family

Mom

Thank you, Mom, because you gave birth to me. You taught me how to be tough and survive rough times because you had a hard life as well. Even though I did not get to live with you my entire life, I have forgiven you for the tough decision that was forced on you when I was sold. I love you very much and always will.

Sisters & Brothers

I thank God that we have reunited after all these years. I am very grateful that we are a family again and that I can come back to Taiwan to see you. Even through all of our challenges, I will always know that you are my sisters and brothers and I love you all very much.

Hannah

You encouraged me to go to church, even being faithful to pick me up, every Sunday, and take me. Especially on those days when I was so tired, you wouldn't give up and for that I am so grateful. It was so worth it!

Thank you for being there and helping me in my freedom, and also for supporting me on my special wedding day.

Mio

Thank you for being my tutor. You had a lot of patience in teaching me the simple things like how to take the bus and even followed the bus to make sure I was alright. I still remember you helping me to order at Taco Bell, to look into people's eyes. It was so much more than just 'tutoring'.

My Faithful Child Care Parents

Thank you for entrusting me with your babies and little children. I love watching each of your children and through them I have found great healing and love.

Fern

Thank you for staying with me for years in the day care. You had confidence in me to care for your sons. I will always be thankful for that. Your friendship and family mean the world to me.

Meg

You have always been there to help me with things that I just couldn't do. I really appreciate all that you have helped me with and for your sons, Ian and Baron.

Mary

You are a very loving and caring person. Thank you for taking care of me when I went through some rough times and supporting me through it.

Lou & Jenna

Thank you for being the first couple to help me when I first got free. I had no one at that time, and you cared about me like a mom and dad. You taught me Chinese and I will always be thankful and you will hold a special place in my heart. My fondest memory is when you took me to Disneyland for the very first time. Thank you for being the pastor who married me.

Andrew

God sent you to me for a special reason. You were there when I first came back to Taiwan, showing me Christian love. You, a fellow Paiwan tribe member, have been unchanging, always supportive—like family to me. You connected me to Elim Publishing and have been such a good friend. Thank you.

Human Trafficking Task Force

Thank you to the Human Trafficking Task Force and The Salvation Army for all your hard work in helping me when I got free. I know I was one of your first cases, but you were there for me and helped me get the support I need in the local survivor's group. I couldn't have made it without you.

...And So Many Others...

Thank you to every single person who was there to help me in my journey to freedom. There are not enough pages in this book to properly thank every single person who was there for me. Know that you are loved and no matter how big or small your contribution, you made a difference in my life and I am forever grateful.

If you suspect a person is a possible victim of human trafficking please call:

National Human Trafficking Hotline

888-373-7888

Sequel to Shari Ho's Story

Finding Freedom
Was Just the Beginning

Available on Amazon

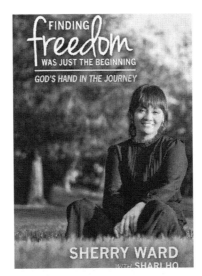

"What happened in Taiwan left me speechless.

What God orchestrated for us—

for Shari—blew me away!"

—Melodie Fox, Author
My Name Is Also Freedom

"Hello Mr. Tree. Do you remember me?" Shari whispered. "I was little girl when you knew me as a slave, but I just wanted to let you know…I'm free now!" The beauty of Shari's favorite tree in its park-like surroundings was in stark contrast to this little girl who was once held as a slave. As Shari continued to speak to the tree, I tried to catch my breath as I looked up at the tree that was cut in the form of a square at the very top. Griped with a new-found sense of God's providence that completely amazed me, I realized that the name of my company Square Tree Publishing was no accident—nor that fact that Shari and I had been brought together by God's design.

Sold as a slave when she was only seven years old, Shari Ho endured much physical and emotional abuse until she got free twenty years later. Little did Shari realize the media fire storm her story would ignite. She would become a beacon of hope to a whole new generation both locally and abroad when she was the focus of the CNN Freedom Report that made headlines all around the word. Her harrowing story is chronicled in the book, *My Name is Also Freedom*.

Finding Freedom was Just the Beginning is a behind-the-scenes look at the making of her book. This four-and half-year journey and a trip to Taiwan, includes all the backstories, miracles, and God-stories that happened along the way. There were so many, they had to be recounted—amazing stories of God's providence intersecting with sheer faith that will keep you on the edge of your seat.

I pray that these God-stories not only inspire you but give you a greater level of faith for your own life. I know that is what Shari would want for you, too.

"As the interpreter for our team in Taiwan,
there were some things you just didn't need to
interpret...like God's tangible presence
in the room."
—Candy Chou
Chinese Interpreter

For more information www.shariho.com.

Available on AMAZON.

At **SQUARE TREE PUBLISHING**, we believe your message matters. That is why our dedicated team of professionals is committed to bringing your literary texts and targeted curriculum to a global marketplace. We strive to make that message of the highest quality, while still maintaining your voice. We believe in you, therefore, we provide a platform through website design, blogs, and social media campaigns to showcase your unique message. Our innovative team offers a full range of services from editing to graphic design inspired with an eye for excellence, so that your message is clearly and distinctly heard.

Whether you are a new writer needing guidance with each step of the process, or a seasoned writer, we will propel you to the next level of your development.

At **SQUARE TREE PUBLISHING**, it's all about **you**.

Take advantage of a free consultation.

Your opportunity is "Write Outside the Box"!

www.SquareTreePublishing.com